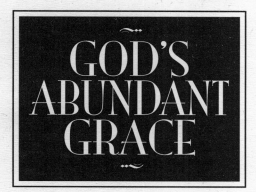

# GOD'S ABUNDANT GRACE

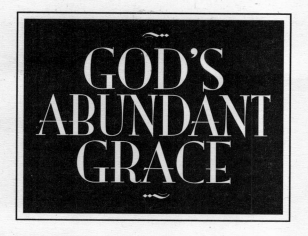

# GOD'S ABUNDANT GRACE

Dwight L. Moody

**MOODY PRESS**
CHICAGO

Updated edition 1998 by
THE MOODY BIBLE INSTITUTE
OF CHICAGO

Originally published in 1891 as *Sovereign Grace* by Fleming
H. Revell.

All Scripture quotations are taken from the King James
Version.

ISBN: 0-8024-5432-1

1 3 5 7 9 10 8 6 4 2

*Printed in the United States of America*

# CONTENTS

Grace! 'Tis a charming sound,
Harmonious to the ear;
Heaven with the echo shall resound,
And all the earth shall hear.

'Twas grace that wrote my name
In life's eternal book;
'Twas grace that gave me to the Lamb;
Who all my sorrows took.

Grace taught my wandering feet
To tread the heavenly road;
And new supplies each hour I meet,
While pressing on to God.

Oh let that grace inspire
My soul with strength divine.
May all my prayers to Thee aspire,
And all my days be Thine.

Dr. Doddridge

# PREFACE

In the exercise of his high calling, the faithful ambassador of Christ must not hesitate to declare the whole counsel of God—"rightly dividing the word of truth" (2 Timothy 2:15)—to all classes of hearers. He must warn the openly wicked man that if he persists in his evil courses, the just judgments of God will inevitably overtake him; he must unmask the hypocrite; he must utter no uncertain protest against the crooked and devious ways of the self-seeker and the time-server. But if he enters into the Spirit of his Master, no part of his public work will be more congenial or delightful than the proclamation of the abundant, sovereign, and free grace of God, manifested towards sinful men in the gift of His eternal Son, to be the Savior of the world.

It has been my happy privilege in years past to tell out, as best I could, this wonderful story of redeeming grace. The following pages record the addresses I have given on the various aspects of this great subject. I pray God that in their printed form they may serve to deepen in the mind of the reader the appreciation of this grace, at once so infinite and so undeserved.

The chapter entitled "A Chime of Gospel Bells," though not strictly flowing out of the general subject, is in perfect harmony with it; every note in the chime is intended to ring out the gracious invitation to come to the God of all grace and be blessed. The Dialogues which form the latter part of the book were heard with much interest and profit at some of the London meetings. I think the perusal of them will be helpful in removing many of the hindrances that prevent anxious inquirers from accepting without delay the salvation that God in His grace has provided for the sinful children of men.

*D. L. Moody.*

# 1
## THE FOUNTAIN OF GRACE

There are some words with which we have been familiar from our infancy up, and probably there are few words in the English language that are so often used as this word *grace*. Many of you at your table "say grace" three times a day. You seldom go into a church without hearing the word mentioned. You seldom read any part of the New Testament, especially the epistles, without meeting the word.

There is probably not a word in the language so little understood. There are a great many who have received the grace of God into their heart but who, if they should be asked what the word means, would be troubled and confused and unable to tell. I experienced the grace of God a good many years before I really knew the true meaning of the word.

Grace means unmerited mercy—undeserved favor. If men were to wake up to the fact, they would not be talking about their own worthiness when we ask them to come to Christ. When the truth dawns upon them that Christ came to save the unworthy, then they will accept salvation. Peter calls God "the God of all grace."

Men talk about grace, but, as a rule, they know very little about it. Let a businessman go to one of your bankers to borrow a few hundred dollars for sixty or ninety days; if he is well able to pay, the banker will perhaps lend him the money if he can get another responsible man to sign the note with him. They give what they call three days' grace after the sixty or ninety days have expired. But they will make the borrower pay interest on the money during these three days, and if he does not return principal and interest at the appointed time, they will sell his goods; they will perhaps turn him out of his house, and take the last piece of furniture in his possession. That is not grace at all; but that fairly illustrates man's idea of it. Grace not only frees you from payment of the interest, but of the principal also.

### Its Source

In the gospel by John we read, "The Word was made flesh and dwelt among us, (and we beheld his glory, the glory as of the only begotten of the Father,) full of grace and truth. . . . For the law was given by Moses, but grace and truth came by Jesus Christ" (John 1:14, 17). Now you know that for many years men were constantly trying to find the source of the Nile. The river of grace has been flowing through this dark earth for six thousand years, and we certainly ought to be more anxious to find out its source than to discover the source of the Nile. I think if you will read your Bible carefully you will find that this wonderful river of grace comes from the very heart of God.

I remember being in Texas a few years ago, in a place where the country was very dry and parched. In that dry country there is a beautiful river that springs right out of the ground. It flows along, and on both sides of the river you find life and vegetation. Grace flows like that river, and you can trace its source right up to the very heart of God. You may say that its highest manifestation was seen when God gave the Son of His bosom to save this lost world. "Not as the offence, so also is the free gift. For if through the offence of one many be dead, much more the grace of God, and the gift by grace, which is by one man, Jesus Christ, hath abounded unto many."

## A Free Gift

Notice, it is the free gift of God. "Grace be unto you, and peace, from God our Father, and from the Lord Jesus Christ. I thank my God always on your behalf, for the grace of God which is given you by Jesus Christ." Paul wrote fourteen epistles; and every one of them is closed with a prayer for grace. Paul calls it "the free gift of God." Thousands have been kept out of the kingdom of God because they do not realize what this free gift is. They think they must do something to merit salvation.

The first promise given to fallen man was a promise of grace. God never promised Adam anything when He put him in Eden. God never entered into a covenant with him as He did with Abraham. God told him, "Of the tree of the knowledge of good and evil, thou shalt not eat of it: for in the day that thou eatest thereof thou shalt surely die"; but when this came to pass, then God came and gave him a gracious promise. He dealt in grace with him. As he left the Garden of Eden he could say to Eve, "Well, God does love us, though He has driven us out."

There was no sign that Adam recognized his lost condition. As far as we know there was no cry for mercy or pardon, no confession of sin. Yet we find that God dealt in grace with him. God sought Adam out that he might bestow His grace upon him. He met Adam in his lost and ruined condition, and the first thing He did was to proclaim the promise of a coming Savior.

For six thousand years, God has been try-ing to teach the world this great and glorious truth—that He wants to deal with man in love and in grace. It runs right through the Bible; all along you find this stream of grace flowing. The very last promise in the closing chapter of Revelation, like the first promise in Eden, is a promise of grace: "Whosoever will, let him take the water of life freely" (Revelation 22:17). So the whole revelation and the whole history of man is encircled with grace, the free favor of God.

Some years ago when I was speaking on this subject, a friend sent me the following: "'By the grace of God I am what I am!' This is the believer's eternal confession. Grace found him a rebel—it leaves him a son. Grace found him wandering at the gates of hell—it leads him through the gates of heaven. Grace devised the scheme of redemption: Justice never would; reason never could. And it is grace which carries out that theme. No sinner would ever have sought his God but 'by grace.' The thickets of Eden would have proved Adam's grave, had not grace called him out. Saul would have lived and died the haughty self-righteous persecutor had not grace laid him low. The thief would have continued breathing out his blasphemies had not grace arrested his tongue and tuned it for glory.

"Out of the knottiest timber," says Rutherford, "He can make vessels of mercy for service in the high palace of glory."

"[Caesar's words] 'I came, I saw, I conquered,'" says Toplady, "may be inscribed by the Savior on every monument of grace." [The Savior can write:] "I came to the sinner; I looked upon him; and with a look of omnipotent love, I conquered."

"My friend, we would have been this day wandering stars, to whom is reserved the blackness of darkness—Christless, hopeless, portionless—had not grace invited us, and grace constrained us," [Rutherford adds].

## Restraining Grace

"Restraining grace," Rutherford says, "is grace that, at this moment, keeps us. We have often been a Peter—forsaking our Lord, but brought back to him again. Why not a Demas or a Judas? 'I have prayed for thee that thy faith fail not.' Is not this our own comment and reflection on life's retrospect? 'Yet not I, but the grace of God which was with me.'"

"Oh, let us seek to realize our continual dependence on this grace every moment! 'More grace! More grace!' should be our continual cry. But the infinite supply is commensurate with the infinite need. The treasury of grace, though always emptying, is always full: the key of prayer which opens it is always at hand: and the almighty [distributor] of the blessings of grace is always waiting to the gracious. The recorded promise never can be canceled or reversed: 'My grace is sufficient for thee.'

"Let us seek to dwell much on this inexhaustible theme. The grace of God is the source of minor temporal as well as of higher spiritual blessings.

"It accounts for the crumb of daily bread as well as for the crown of eternal glory. But even in regard to earthly mercies, never forget the channel of grace through Christ Jesus. It is sweet thus to connect every (even the smallest and humblest) token of providential bounty with Calvary's Cross—to have the common blessings of life, tamped with the print of the nails. It makes them doubly precious to think this flows from Jesus. Let others be contented with the uncovenanted mercies of God. Be it ours to say as the children of grace and heirs of glory: 'Our Father which art in heaven, give us this day our daily bread.' Nay, reposing in the all-sufficiency in all things, promised by the God of all grace."

# 2

## SAVED BY GRACE ALONE

I want to call your attention to the fact that we are saved by grace alone, not by works *and* grace. A great many people think that they can be saved by works. Others think that salvation may be attained by works and grace together. They need to have their eyes opened to see that the gift of God is free and apart from works.

"For by grace are ye saved through faith; and that not of yourselves: it is the gift of God: not of works, lest any man should boast" (Ephesians 2:8–9). Many people would put it thus: "For by your works are ye saved—or by your tears, or your prayers, or your fastings, or your trials, or your good resolutions, or your money!" But Paul tells us plainly that it is "not of works, lest any man should boast." If we could be saved by works, then of course Christ's mission to this world was a mistake. There was no need for Him to come.

What had Paul ever done that could merit salvation? Up to the time that Christ called him he had done everything he could against Christ and against Christianity. He was in the very act of going to Damascus to cast into prison every Christian he could find. If he had not been stopped, many of them would probably have been put to death. It was Paul, remember, who cheered on the mob that stoned Stephen. Yet we find that when Christ met him He dealt in grace with him. No apostle says so much against salvation by works *before* the Cross, as Paul; and none says so much about works *after* the Cross. He put works in their right place. I have very little sympathy with any man who has been redeemed by the precious blood of the Son of God and who has not got the spirit of work. If we are children of God, we ought not to have a lazy drop of blood in our veins. If a man tells me that he has been saved and does not desire to work for the honor of God, I doubt his salvation. Laziness belongs to the old creation, not to the new. In all my experience I never knew a lazy man to be converted —never. I have more hope of the salvation of drunkards, and thieves, and harlots, than of a lazy man.

## What the Thirty-Nine Articles Say

Some people have accused me of teaching heresy, because I say salvation is all of grace. I remember a clergyman once said I was teaching false doctrine because I said salvation was all of grace. He said that works had as much to do with our salvation as grace. At that time I had never read the Thirty-Nine Articles. If I had I would have been ready to meet him. I got the Prayer Book and looked through the Thirty-Nine Articles; and I found, to my amazement, that they put it a good deal stronger than I had done. Let us hear what three of them say:

"*XI. Of the Justification of Man.* We are accounted righteous before God, only for the merit of our Lord and Savior Jesus Christ by Faith, and not for our own works or deservings: Wherefore, that we are justified by Faith only, is a most wholesome doctrine, and very full of comfort."

"*XII. Of Good Works.* Albeit that Good Works, which are the fruits of Faith and follow after Justification, cannot put away our sins, and endure the severity of God's judgment; yet are they pleasing and acceptable to God in Christ, and do spring out necessarily of a true and lively Faith; insomuch that by them a lively Faith may be as evidently known as a tree discerned by the fruit."

"*XIII. Of Works Before Justification.* Works done before the grace of Christ, and the inspiration of His Spirit, are not pleasant to God; forasmuch as they spring not of faith in Jesus Christ, neither do they make men meet to receive grace, or (as the school authors say) deserve grace of congruity: yea rather, for that they are not done as God hath willed and commanded them to be done, we doubt not but they have the nature of sin."

That is stronger than I ever put it. These

Articles say of works before justification that "they have the nature of *sin*." I never called them sin! So you see this is not any new doctrine that we are preaching. When the church and the world wake up to the fact that works before salvation go for naught, then—and not till then, I believe—men will come flocking into the kingdom of God by hundreds. We work from the Cross, not to it. We work because we are saved, not in order to be saved. We work from salvation, not up to it. Salvation is the gift of God.

You have heard the Prayer Book. Now hear Paul: "Abraham believed God, and it was counted unto him for righteousness. Now to him that worketh is the reward not reckoned of grace, but of debt. But to him that worketh not, but believeth on him that justifieth the ungodly, his faith is counted for righteousness" (Romans 4:3–5). Notice what the apostle says: "to him that worketh not." That is plain language, is it not? I may perhaps startle some of you by saying that many of you have been kept out of the kingdom of God by your good works. Nevertheless it is true. If you put works in the place of faith, they become a snare to you. It is "to him that worketh not, but believeth."

I freely admit salvation is worth working for; it is worth a man's going round the world on his hands and knees, climbing its mountains, crossing its valleys, swimming its rivers, going through all manner of hardship in order to attain. But we do not get it in that way. Paul went through all the trials and hardships he had to endure, because by the grace of God resting on him he was enabled to do so.

### Penance for Sin

Would you insult the Almighty by offering Him the fruits of this frail body to atone for sin? Supposing your queen were to send me a magnificent present, and I said to the royal messenger: "I certainly should not like to accept this from Her Majesty without giving her something in return." Suppose I should send her a penny! How would the queen feel, if I were to insult her in that way? And what have we that we can offer to God in return for His free gift of salvation? Less than nothing. We must come and take salvation in God's way.

There is no merit in taking a gift. If a beggar comes to my house, and asks for bread to eat, and I give him a loaf of bread, there is no merit in his taking the bread. So if you experience the favor of God, you have to take it as a beggar. Someone has said: "If you come to God as a prince, you go away as a beggar; if you come as a beggar, you go away as a prince." It is to the needy that God opens the wardrobe of heaven, and brings out the robe of righteousness.

Paul says again: "If by grace, then is it no more of works: otherwise grace is no more grace. But if it be of works, then is it no more grace: otherwise work is no more work." Paul is reasoning in this way, that if I work for a gift or attempt to give money for it, it ceases to be a gift. The only way to get a gift is to take it as a gift.

An old man got up in one of our meetings and said, "I have been forty-two years learning three things." I pricked up my ears at that. I thought that if I could find out in about three minutes what a man had taken forty-two years to learn I should like to do it. The first thing he said he had learned was that he could do nothing towards his own salvation. "Well," said I to myself, "that is worth learning." The second thing he had found out was that God did not require him to do anything. Well, that was worth finding out too. And the third thing was that the Lord Jesus Christ had done it all; salvation was finished, and that all he had to do was to take it. Dear friends, let us learn this lesson; let us give up our struggling and striving, and accept salvation at once.

### A Free Pardon

I was preaching in the southern states a few years ago, and the minister called my attention to one of the elders in his church. He said, "When the Civil War broke out, that man was in one of the far Southern states, and he enlisted into the Southern army. He was selected by the Southern general as a spy and sent to spy out the Northern army. As you know, armies have no mercy on spies, if they can catch them. This man was caught. He was tried by court-martial and ordered to be shot. While he was in the guardroom previous to the time of execution, the Northern soldiers used to bring him his rations. Every time they came to his cell he would call Abraham Lincoln by every vile epithet he could think of. It seemed as though he 'lay awake nights,' trying to study such names. At last the soldiers got so angry that they said they would be glad when the bullet went through his heart. Some of them even said they would like to put a bullet through him, and if they were not obliged by military order to feed him, they would let him starve in the prison. They thought that was what he deserved for talking so unjustly of Lincoln.

"One day while the man was in the prison, waiting to be led out to execution, a Northern officer came to the cell. The prisoner, full of rage, thought his time was come to be shot. The officer opened the prison door, and handed him a free pardon from Abraham Lincoln. He told him he was at liberty: he could go to his wife and children! The man who had before been so full of bitterness and malice and rage suddenly quieted down and said, 'What, has Abraham Lincoln pardoned me! For what? I never said a good word about him.' The officer said, 'If you had what you deserved you would be shot. But someone interceded for you at Washington and obtained your pardon; you are now at liberty.'"

The minister, as he told me, said that this act of undeserved kindness quite broke the man's heart and led to his conversion. Said the minister, "You let any man speak one word against Abraham Lincoln now in the hearing of that man and see what will happen. There is not a man in all the Republic of America, I believe, who has a kinder feeling towards our late president than he."

Now that is grace. The man did not *deserve* a pardon. But this is exactly what grace is: *undeserved mercy*. You may have been a rebel against God up to this very hour; but if you acknowledge your rebellion and are willing to take the mercy that God offers, you can have it freely. It is there for every soul on the face of the earth. "The grace of God that bringeth salvation hath appeared to all men." Thank God for that! Salvation by grace is for all men. If we are lost, it will not be because God has not provided a Savior, but because we spurn the gift of God— because we dash the cup of salvation from us.

What says Christ? You remember that when He was on earth, they came to Him and asked what they should do to work the works of God. He had been telling them to labor not for the bread that perisheth, but for the meat that endureth unto everlasting life.

Then they asked Him, "What shall we do that we may work the works of God?" What did Jesus tell them to do? Did He tell them to go and feed the hungry, to clothe the naked, to visit the widow and the fatherless in their affliction? Perhaps you may say that, according to Scripture, is "pure and undefiled religion." Granted; but something comes before that. That is all right and necessary in its place. But when these men wanted to know what they had to do to inherit eternal life, Jesus said: "This is the work of God, that ye believe on him whom he hath sent."

## You Can Believe

A friend lately called my attention to the fact that God has put the offer of salvation in such a way that the whole world can lay hold of it. All men can believe. A lame man might not perhaps be able to visit the sick; but he can believe. A blind man by reason of his infirmity cannot do many things; but he can believe. A deaf man can believe. A dying man can believe. God has put salvation so simply that the young and the old, the wise and the foolish, the rich and the poor can all believe if they will.

Do you think that Christ would have come down from heaven, would have gone to Gethsemane and to Golgotha, would have suffered as He did, if man could have worked his way up to heaven—if he could have merited salvation by his own efforts? I think if you give five minutes' consideration to this question you will see that if man could have saved himself Christ need not have suffered at all. Remember, too, what Christ says. "He . . . that climbeth up some other way, the same is a thief and a robber" (John 10:1). He has marked out the way to God. He has opened up a new and shining way, and He wants us to take His way. Certainly the attempt to work our way up to heaven is "climbing up some other way," is it not? If ever a man did succeed in working his way into heaven we should never hear the last of it! I have got so terribly sick of these so-called "self-made men." There are some men whom you cannot approach without hearing them blow their trumpet, saying, "I am a self-made man. I came here a poor man ten years ago, and now I am rich." It is all I—I—I! They go on boasting, and telling what wonderful beings they are! There is one thing that is excluded from the kingdom of heaven, and that is boasting. If you and I ever get there it will be by the sovereign grace of God. There will be no credit due ourselves.

> "Saved by grace alone
>  This is all my plea:
>  Jesus died for all mankind,
>  And Jesus died for me."

# 3

## POSSESSING AND "WORKING OUT"

I can imagine someone asking: What does that passage mean: "Work out your own salvation with fear and trembling" (Philippians 2:12)? Well, I want to emphasize the word *your:* "Work out *your* salvation." That is most important. You hear people talk of working out salvation, when all the time they have not got it. How can you work out what you do not possess? Paul is here writing to the Christians at Philippi. They were already saved by the grace of God. Now that they had got this wonderful gift, he says: "Go, work it out."

When you see a person working for salvation, you may know that he has got a false idea of the teaching of the Scripture. We have salvation as a gift; and of course we cannot get it by working for it. It is our appreciation of this gift that makes us work.

Many people are working and working, as Rowland Hill says, like children on a rocking horse—it is a beautiful motion, but there is no progress. Those who are working for salvation are like men on a treadmill, going round and round and round, toiling and toiling and toiling; but nothing comes of it all. There is no progress, and there cannot be until you have the motive power within, till the breath of life comes from God, who alone can give you power to work for others.

Suppose I say to my son: "You are going away from home; and I want you to be very careful how you spend that $500." "Well," he says, "if you will give me $500, I will be careful about it; but how can I be careful in spending what I have not got?" And so, unless you have salvation, you cannot work it out.

Take another illustration. One summer my boy asked me to give him a piece of ground that he might have a garden all to himself. I said I would give it to him but that I expected he would keep it clear of weeds, and use it in some way that would make it pleasant and profitable to him. He was to work out the piece of land; but he could not do that until I had given it to him. Neither was it his working it out that secured him the garden. I gave it to him freely, apart from any merit of his own; but I did so on the understanding that he should employ it to the best advantage. I think that is a fair illustration of our working out the salvation that God has given us.

Of course these illustrations fail in some points. I could not impart to my son the willingness to work out the piece of land, though I could provide him with all the necessary implements. God not only gives us salvation freely, but He gives us the power to work it out.

A writer says on this point: "Paul does not command the Philippians *to save themselves*. There was no thought in his mind of any meritorious self-righteousness. Man can by no work of his own either procure salvation or merit salvation. God worketh the salvation within the soul—man only worketh that salvation out in the Christian life. To break off from known sin; to renounce all self-righteousness; to cast ourselves in loving faith on the merits of Christ crucified; to commence at once a life of self-denial, of prayer, of obedience; to turn from all that God forbids, resolutely and earnestly, unto all that God requires—this is what the text implies. But then this is not salvation. Salvation is of God—of grace—of free grace.

"From the germ to the fruit, from foundation to the top stone it is of grace, free grace, altogether and only. But the working out of salvation is man's part in the work of salvation. God will not repent for the man; nor believe for the man; nor lead a holy life for the man. God worketh inwardly—man worketh outwardly. And this outward human work is as necessary as the inward Divine work."

*God works in us,* and then we work *for* Him. If He has done a work in us, we certainly ought to go and work for others. A man must have this salvation and must know it, before he can work for the salvation of others.

Many of you have tried hard to save yourselves; but what has been the end of it all? I remember a lady in the north of England who became quite angry when I made this remark publicly: "No one in this congregation will be saved till they stop trying to save themselves." Down she came from the gallery, and said to me: "You have made me perfectly miserable." "Indeed," I said, "how is that?"

"Why, I always thought that if I kept on trying, God would save me at some time; and now you tell me to stop trying: what, then, am I to do?"

"Why, let the Lord save you."

She went off in something like a rage. It is not always a bad sign when you see a man or a woman wake up cross, if it is the Word of God that wakes them up. A day or two afterwards she came and thanked me. She said she had been turning over in her mind what I had said; and at last the truth dawned upon her, that though she had worked long, though she had formed a good many resolutions, she had made no progress. So she gave up the struggle; and then it was that the Lord Jesus saved her.

I want to ask you this question: If sin needs forgiveness—and all sin is against God—how can you work out your own forgiveness? If I stole $100 from a friend, I could not forgive myself, could I? No act of mine would bring about forgiveness, unless my friend forgave me. And so, if I want forgiveness of sin, it must be the work of God. If we look at salvation as a new life, it must be the work of God. God is the author of life. You cannot give yourself life. If we consider it as a gift, it must come from someone outside of ourselves. That is what I read in the Bible—salvation is a gift. While I am speaking, you can make up your mind that you will stop trying and take this gift.

I wish I could get this whole audience to drop the word *try*, and put the word *trust* in its place. The forgiving grace of God is wonderful. He will save you this very minute, if you are willing to be saved. He delights in mercy. He wants to show that mercy to every soul. The religion of Christ is not man working his way up to God; it is God coming down to man. It is Christ coming down to the pit of sin and woe where we are, bringing us out of the pit, putting our feet upon a rock, and a new song in our mouth. He will do it this minute, while I am speaking, if you will let Him. Will you let Him? That is the question.

I do not believe much in dreams, but they sometimes illustrate a point. I heard about a woman who had been trying for a long time, just like many of you, to be better and better. She tried to save herself, but made no progress. One night she fell asleep in a very troubled state of mind, and she had a dream. She thought that she was in a pit striving to get out: climbing and slipping, climbing and slipping, climbing and slipping. At last she gave up the struggle, and laid herself down at the bottom of the pit to die.

She happened to look up, and she saw through the mouth of the pit a beautiful star. She fixed her eye on it; and it seemed as if the star lifted her up till she was almost out. But the thought of herself came to her mind; she looked off at the sides of the pit: immediately she lost sight of the star, and down to the bottom of the pit she went. Again she fixed her eye on the star; and again it seemed to lift her almost out. But once again she took her eye off the star and looked at herself; down into the pit she fell again! The third time she fixed her eye on the star and was lifted higher and higher, until all at once her feet struck the ground above, and she awoke from her sleep.

God taught her a lesson by the dream. She learned that if ever she was to be saved, she must give up the struggle, and let Jesus Christ save her. My friends, give up the struggle today! You have tried long and hard. It has been a hard battle, has it not? Give it up and repose in the arms of Jesus Christ. Say "Lord, I come to thee as a poor sinner; wilt Thou not save me and help me?" He will. "The gift of God is eternal life." It is offered to all who will have it.

I see some children here; let me tell you a story. If you have not heard it before, please do not forget it. A Sunday school teacher wished to show his class how free the gift of God is. He took a silver watch from his pocket one day and offered it to the eldest boy in the class. "It is yours, if you will take it." The little fellow sat and grinned at the teacher. He thought he was joking. The teacher offered it to the next boy, and said: "Take that watch: it is yours." The little fellow thought he would be laughed at if he held out his hand, and therefore he sat still. In the same way the teacher went nearly round the class, but not one of them would accept the proffered gift.

At length he came to the smallest boy. When the watch was offered to the little fellow, he took it and put it into his pocket. All the class laughed at him. "I am thankful, my boy," said the teacher, "that you believe my word. The watch is yours. Take good care of it. Wind it up every night."

The rest of the class looked on in amazement; and one of them said: "Teacher, you don't mean that the watch is his? You don't mean that he doesn't have to give it back to you?" "No," said the teacher, "he does not have to give it back to me. It is his own now."

"Ohhh! If I had only known that, I would have taken it!"

I see you laugh; but my friends, you are

laughing at yourselves. You need not go far away to find these boys. Salvation is freely offered to all, but the trouble is that men do not believe God's Word, and do not accept the gift. Who will accept it now?

I found a few lines the other day on this point and thought them very good. I will close with them:

> I would not work my soul to save,
> For that my Lord hath done;
> But I would work like any slave,
> For love of God's dear Son.

# 4

## GRACE ABOUNDING TO THE CHIEF OF SINNERS

I want to emphasize that God desires to show mercy to all. Christ's last command to His disciples was, "Go ye into all the world, and preach the gospel to every creature." There may be some hearing me who have not received this grace, though it has often been pressed on their acceptance. One reason why many do not become partakers of this grace is that they think they can do better without it. The Jews said they were the seed of Abraham. They had Moses and the Law: therefore they had no need of the pardoning grace of God that Christ had come to bring. We read in the book of Revelation of a church that said it was "rich, and increased with goods, and [had] need of nothing." That was the trouble when Christ was down here. Instead of coming to Him to be blessed, the people too often went away thinking and saying they had no need of His favor and blessing.

### The Two Prayers

In the gospel by Luke Christ brings two men before us. I do not know that we can find

any two cases in Scripture that will give us more
light on this subject than those of the Pharisee
and the publican, who went into the temple to
pray. One went away as empty as he came. He
was like the church described in Revelation, to
which I have referred. He went into the temple
desiring nothing; and he got nothing. The
other man asked for something; he asked for
pardon and mercy. And he went down to his
house justified. Take the prayer of the Pharisee. There is no confession in it, no adoration,
no contrition, no petition. As I have said, he
asked for nothing and he got nothing. Someone has said that he went into the temple not
to pray but to boast.

The sun and the moon were as far apart as
these two men. One was altogether of a different spirit to the other. The one prayed with his
head, and the other with his heart. The one
told God what a wonderfully great and good
man he was: "I am not as other men—or even
as this publican." His prayer was not a long
one; it consisted of thirty-four words, yet there
were five capital "I's" in it. It was self in the
beginning, self in the middle, self in the end—
self all through. "I fast twice a week"; "I give
tithes of all I possess"; "I am a wonderfully
good man, am I not, Lord?" He struck a bal-
ance twice a week, and God was his debtor
every time. He paraded his good deeds before

God and man. Such a one was not in a condition to receive the favor of God.

You can divide the human family today into two classes—Pharisees and publicans. There are those who are poor in spirit; the dew of God's grace will fall upon them. There are others who are drawing around them the rags of their self-righteousness; they will always go away without the blessing of God. There were but seven words in the prayer of the Publican: "God be merciful to me a sinner!" He came to God confessing his sins, and asking for mercy; and he received it.

If you were to run through Scripture, you would find that where men have gone to God in the spirit of the publican, God has dealt with them in mercy and grace.

A young man came to one of our meetings in New York a few years ago. He was convicted of sin; and he made up his mind he would go home and pray. He lived a number of miles away, and he started for home. On the way, as he was meditating about his sins and wondering what he was going to do when he got home, the thought occurred to him: "Why should I not pray right here in the street?" But he found he did not know just how to begin. Then he remembered that when he was a child, his mother had taught him this prayer of the publican: "God be merciful to me a sinner!" So he began just where he stood. He said afterward that before he got to the little word "me," God met him in grace, and blessed him. And so the moment we open our lips to ask God for pardon, if the request comes from the heart, God will meet us in mercy.

Let our cry be that of the publican: "Be merciful to me"—not to someone else. A mother was telling me some time ago that she had trouble with one of her sons because he had not treated his brother rightly. She sent him upstairs; and after a while she asked him what he had been doing. He replied that he had been *praying for his brother!* Although he had been the naughty one, he was acting as if the fault lay with his brother instead of himself. So many of us can see the failings of others readily enough; but when we get a good look at ourselves, we will get down before God as the publican did and cry for mercy and that cry will bring an immediate answer.

God delights to deal in grace with the poor in spirit. He wants to see in us a broken and contrite heart. If we take the place of a sinner, confessing our sins and asking for mercy, the grace of God will meet us right then and there; and we shall have the assurance of His forgiveness.

In Matthew we see how God deals in grace with those who come in the right spirit. "Then came she and worshipped him, saying, Lord, help me! But he answered and said, It is not meet to take the children's bread, and to cast it to dogs. And she said, Truth, Lord: yet the dogs eat of the crumbs which fall from their masters' table. Then Jesus answered and said unto her, O woman, great is thy faith: be it unto thee even as thou wilt. And her daughter was made whole from that very hour" (Matthew 15:25–28).

The disciples did not understand how full of grace was the heart of Christ. This poor woman belonged to the far-off coasts of Tyre and Sidon. She was a poor Gentile, and they wanted to send her away. They thought she was not one of the elect; she did not belong to the house of Israel. So they said to the Master, "Send her away; for she crieth after us." Can you conceive of the loving Savior sending away a poor troubled one who comes to Him? I challenge you to find a single instance of His doing such a thing, from the beginning to the end of His ministry. "Send her away!" I believe He would rather send an angel away than a poor suppliant for His mercy. He delighted to have one such as she come to Him. But He was going to test her, as well as to give an object lesson to those who should come after. "It is not meet," He said, "to take the children's bread, and to cast it to dogs."

## A Humble Spirit

I am afraid if some of us had been in her place we would have answered somewhat in this fashion: "You call me a Gentile dog, do you? I would not take anything from you now if you were to give it to me." If this poor woman had replied to the Master in such a fashion, she would not have got anything. Yet you will find a good many men who respond to the Savior in that way when He wants to deal in grace with them.

What does this Gentile woman say? "Truth, Lord: yet the dogs eat of the crumbs which fall from their masters' table." She took her right place—down at the feet of the blessed Master. There was humility for you and I. She was willing to take any place if the Lord would but meet her need; and the Lord blessed her. She asked for a crumb, and He gave her a whole loaf.

I once heard Rev. William Arnot say that he was the guest of a friend who had a favorite dog. The animal would come into the room where the family were sitting at the dinner table and would stand looking at his master. If the master threw him a crumb, the dog would seize it before it got to the floor. But if he put the joint of meat down on the floor the dog would look at it and leave it alone, as if it were too good for him.

"So," said Mr. Arnot, "there are many Christians who are satisfied to live on crumbs, when God wants to give them the whole joint."

### A Full Blessing

This poor woman got all she wanted, and if we will come in the right spirit—if we are humble and poor in spirit—and call upon God for what we want, He will not disappoint us. She went right to the Son of God and appealed to His great loving heart with the cry, "Lord, help me!" and he helped her. Let that cry go up to Him today and see how quickly the answer will come. I never knew a case where God did not answer right on the spot when there was the spirit of meekness. If, on the other hand, we are conceited and think we have a right to come, putting ourselves on an equality with God, we shall get nothing.

### "Worthiness"

In the gospel by Luke we read of the centurion who had a sick servant. He felt as though he were not worthy to go himself and ask Christ to come to his house, so he asked some of his friends to beseech the Master to come and heal his servant. They went and delivered the centurion's message, saying, "He was worthy for whom he should do this: for he loveth our nation, and he hath built us a synagogue" (Luke 7:4–5). The Jews could not understand grace; so they thought Christ would grant the request of this man because he was worthy. "Why," they said, "he hath built us a synagogue!" It is the same old story that we hear today. Let a man give a few thousand dollars to build a church, and he must have the best pew; "he is worthy." Perhaps he made his money by selling or making strong drink: but he has put the church under an obligation by this gift of money, and he is considered "worthy." The same spirit was at work in the days of Christ.

The Master immediately started for the centurion's house, and it looked as though He were going because of his personal worthiness. But if He had done so, it would have upset the whole story as an illustration of grace. As the Savior was on the way, out came the Roman officer himself and told Jesus that he was not worthy to receive Him under his roof. He had a very different opinion of himself to that of his Jewish friends. Suppose he had said, "Lord, you will be my guest. Come and heal my servant because I am worthy: I have built a synagogue." Do you think Christ would have come? I do not think He would. But he said, "I am not worthy that thou shouldest enter under my roof: . . . but say in a word, and my servant shall be healed."

Jesus marveled at the man's faith. It pleased Him wonderfully to find such faith and humility. Like the Syro-Phoenician woman, he had low thoughts of himself and high thoughts of God; therefore he was in a condition to receive the grace of God. His servant, we are told, was healed that very hour. His petition was granted at once. Let us learn a lesson from this man, and take a humble position before God, crying to Him for mercy. Then help will come.

## Great Forgiveness

I never noticed till lately an interesting fact about the story of the poor sinful woman mentioned in Luke's gospel, who went into Simon's house. The incident occurred immediately after Christ had uttered those memorable words we read in Matthew: "Come unto me, all ye that labour and are heavy laden, and I will give you rest" (11:28). Matthew closes the narrative there; but in the seventh chapter of Luke you will find what the result of that invitation was. A poor fallen woman came into the house where He was and obtained the blessing of rest to her soul. I think that many ministers will bear me out in this statement that when one has preached to a large congregation and has given an invitation to those who would like to remain and talk about salvation, probably the only one to do so is a poor fallen one, who will thus become a partaker of the grace of God.

We find that the Savior was invited to the house of Simon, a Pharisee. While He was there, this poor sinful woman crept into the house. Perhaps she watched for a chance when the servants were away from the door and then slipped into the room where the Master was. She got down on her knees and began to wash His feet with her tears, wiping them with the hairs of her head. While the feast was going on the Pharisee saw this; and he said to himself: "Jesus must be a bad man, if He knows who this poor woman is." Even if Jesus did not know, He would be unclean according to the Mosaic law, because He had allowed the woman to touch Him. But the Master knew what Simon was thinking about. He put some questions to him: "And Jesus answering said unto him, Simon, I have somewhat to say unto thee. And he saith, Master, say on. There was a certain creditor which had two debtors: the one owed five hundred pence, and the other fifty. And when they had nothing to pay, he frankly forgave them both. Tell me therefore, which of them will love him most? Simon answered and said, I suppose that he, to whom he forgave most. And he said unto him, Thou hast rightly judged" (Luke 7:40–43).

Then He made the application: In Simon's house Jesus received "no water for [His] feet . . . no kiss" or oil for His head. "You refused me the common hospitalities of life," Jesus said. In those days when one went into a gentleman's house, a servant would be at the door with a basin of water; the guest would slip off his sandals, and the servant would wash his feet. Then the master of the house would salute him with a kiss instead of shaking hands as we do. There would also be oil for his head. Christ had been invited to Simon's house, but the Pharisee had got Him there in a patronizing spirit.

"You gave me no water, no kiss, no oil; but this woman hath washed my feet with her tears, and wiped them with the hairs of her head," Jesus told Simon. "She hath not ceased to kiss my feet, and she hath anointed them with ointment. She was forgiven much: and so she loves much." To the poor woman herself Jesus said, "Thy sins are forgiven" (verse 48). They may have risen up like a dark mountain before her, but one word from the Savior and they were all gone.

The spirit shown by Simon was altogether different from that of the poor woman. Christ said that the publicans and harlots would go into the kingdom of God before the self-righteous Pharisees! Simon, the Pharisee, got nothing; and so there are many who go away from religious meetings without one drop of heaven's dew, because they do not seek for it. From the morning of the creation down to the present time no man or woman ever went to God with a broken heart without experiencing the forgiving love and grace of God, if they believed His Word. It was so with this poor woman. Notice, the Master did not extract any pledge or promise from her. He did not ask her to join some synagogue; all He said was, "Thy sins are forgiven." She found grace. So it was with the Syro-Phoenician woman. Christ did not ask any pledge from her: He met her in grace, and blessed her according to her soul's desire.

You know what touched the heart of the father of the prodigal; it was the broken and contrite spirit of his returning son. Would not the same thing move the heart of any parent here? Suppose you had a son who had gone astray; the boy comes home; and when you meet him, he begins to confess his sin. Would you not take him to your bosom and forgive him? Nothing in the wide world would you more readily do than forgive him. So if we come to God with this contrite spirit, He will deal in grace with us and receive us freely. When Saul left Jerusalem, there was nothing he wished for less than to receive the grace of God. Yet the moment he said, "Lord, what wilt thou have me to do?" the forgiving grace of the Master flowed out toward him. We are told by Matthew and Mark that the thief on the cross, who was converted, railed on the Savior at first like the other; but the very moment his heart was broken down and he said, "Lord, remember me!" Christ heard and answered his prayer.

God is waiting to cover all your sins today; He has a long and a strong arm that can reach down to the darkest, vilest, deepest depths of sin. He will lift you up on a rock, and put a new song into your mouth. Will you let Him do it ?

A man was telling me some time ago that he had prayed for over ten years that God would have mercy upon him. "Has not God answered your prayer?"

"No."

"Indeed! Let me ask you one question. Suppose I offered you that Bible as a gift, and you were afterward to come and ask me for it; what would I think of you?"

"I do not know what you would think."

"Well, but what do you suppose I would think?"

"You would perhaps think I had gone a little wrong in my head."

"What is the use of your asking that God would deal in grace with you," I said, "if you are not willing to receive it, or if you do not believe that He gives it to you?"

When I was on the Pacific Coast some years ago, I stayed with a friend who had a large garden, with a great many orange trees. He said to me: "Make yourself perfectly at home. If you see anything you want, just help yourself." When I wanted some oranges, I did not go into the garden and pray to the oranges to tumble into my mouth; I just put out my hand and took all I required. So it is with us. Why should we go on asking and beseeching God to have mercy upon us, when He has already given His Son, and given His Holy Spirit? What we need is to have a broken and contrite heart, and to be willing to receive Him. The trouble with us is that we have locked the doors of our hearts against Him.

There is a story that Dr. Arnot was accustomed to tell of a poor woman who was in great distress because she could not pay her landlord his rent. The doctor put some money in his pocket and went round to the house, intending to help her. When he got there, he knocked at the door. He thought he heard some movement inside; but no one came to open the door. He knocked louder and louder still; but yet no one came. Finally he kicked at the door, causing some of the neighbors to look out and see what was going on. But he could get no entrance; and at last he went away thinking his ears must have deceived him, and that there was really no one there. A day or two afterwards he met the woman in the street, and told her what had happened. She held up her hands and exclaimed, "Was that you? I was in the house all the while; but I thought it was the landlord, and I had the door locked!"

Many people are keeping the door of their heart locked against the Savior in just the same way. They say, "I am afraid I shall have to give up so much." That is something like a ragged beggar being unwilling to give up his rags, in order to get a new suit of good clothes. I pity those people who are all the time fooling themselves to see what they will have to give up. God wants to bestow His marvelous grace on His people; and there is not a soul who has believed on Jesus, for whom God has not abundant grace in store. What would you say of a man dying of thirst on the banks of a beautiful river, with the stream flowing past his feet? You could think he was mad! The river of God's grace flows on without ceasing; why should we not partake of it, and go on our way rejoicing?

Do you say you are sinners? It is just to such as you that God's grace is given. There was a sailor whose mother had long been praying for him. I do think mothers' prayers are sure to be answered some day. One night the memory of his mother came home to this man; he thought of the days of his childhood, and he made up his mind he would try and lead a different life. When he got to New York he thought he would join the Odd-Fellows; he imagined that would be a good way to begin. What miserable mistakes men make when they get trying to save themselves! This man applied to a lodge of Odd-Fellows for admission; but the committee found that he was a drinking man, and so they blackballed him. Then he thought he would try the Freemasons; they discovered what sort of a man he was, and they blackballed him too.

One day he was walking along Fulton Street, when he received an invitation to come to the daily prayer meeting held there. He went in and heard about the Savior; he received Christ into his heart, and found the peace and power he wanted. Some days after he stood up in the meeting and told the story: how the Odd-Fellows had blackballed him; how the Freemasons had blackballed him; and how he came to the Lord Jesus Christ, who had not blackballed him, but took him right in. That is what Christ will do to every poor penitent sinner. "This Man receiveth sinners." Come to Him today, and He will receive you: His abundant, sovereign grace will cover and put away all your sins.

I am so glad that we have a Savior who can save unto the very uttermost. He can save the drunkard, the man who for years has been the slave of his passions. I was talking to a friend not long ago, who said that if a man had a father and a mother who were drunkards, he would inherit the taste for drink, and that there was not much chance of saving him. I want to say that there is a grand chance for such men, if they will call upon Jesus Christ to save them. He is able to destroy the very appetite for drink. He came to destroy the works of the devil; and if this appetite for gin and whiskey is not the work of the devil, I want to know what is. I do not know any more terrible agency that the devil has got than this intoxicating liquor.

An Englishman went out from England to Chicago, and became one of the greatest drunkards in that city. His father and his mother were drunkards before him. He said that when he was four years old, his father took him into a public house and put the liquor to his lips. By and by he got a taste for it; and for several years he was a confirmed drunkard. He became what in America we call a "tramp." He slept out-of-doors. One night, on the shore of a lake, he awoke from his slumber, and began to call upon God to save him. There at the midnight hour, this poor, wretched, forlorn object got victory over his sin.

The last time I met him he had been nine and one-half years a sober man. From that memorable midnight hour, he said, he had never had any desire to touch or taste strong drink. God had kept him all those years. I am so thankful we have a Gospel that we can carry into the home of the drunkard, and tell him that Christ will save him. That is the very thing He came to do.

John Bunyan represents the power of grace, as shown by its first offer to the Jerusalem sinners, . . . thus: "Repent, and be baptized every one of you, in the name of Jesus Christ for the remission of sins, and ye shall receive gift of the Holy Ghost" (Acts 2:38).

"But I was one of those who plotted to take away His life. May I be saved by Him?"

*"Every one of you."*

"But I was one of those who bore false witness against Him. Is there grace for me?"

For *"every one of you."*

"But I was one of those who cried out, 'Crucify Him! Crucify Him!' and who desired that Barabbas, the murderer, might live, rather than He. What will become of me, think you?"

"I am to preach repentance and remission of sins to *every one of you.*"

"But I was one of those who did spit in His face when He stood before His accusers; I also was one who mocked Him when, in anguish, He hung bleeding on the tree. Is there room for me?"

For *"every one of you."*

"But I was one of those who, in His extremity, said, 'Give Him gall and vinegar to drink!' Why may I not expect the same when pain and anguish are upon me?"

"Repent of these thy wickednesses; and here is remission of sins for *every one of you.*"

"But I railed on Him; I reviled Him; I hated Him. I rejoiced to see Him mocked at by others. Can there be hope for me?"

"There is; for *every one of you.*"

Oh, what a blessing *every one of you* is here. How willing was Peter—and the Lord Jesus by the ministry of Peter—to catch these murderers with the word of the Gospel, that they might be monuments to the grace of God!

Now it is a solemn fact that everyone who receives the offer of the Gospel can lock and bolt the door to his heart, and say to the Lord Jesus Christ that he refuses to let Him in. But it is also a blessed truth that you can unlock that door and say to Him, "Welcome, thrice welcome, Son of God, into this heart of mine!" The question is: Will you let Christ come in and save you? It is not a question of whether He is able. Who will open their hearts, and let the Savior come in?

"There's a stranger at the door:
Let Him in!
He has been there oft before:
Let Him in!
Let Him in, ere He is gone;
Let Him in, the Holy One,
Jesus Christ, the Father's Son:
Let Him in!

"Open now to Him your heart:
Let Him in!
If you wait He will depart:
Let Him in!
Let Him in, He is your Friend.
He your soul will sure defend.
He will keep you to the end.
Let Him in!

"Hear you now His loving voice?
Let Him in!
Now, oh now, make Him your choice:
Let Him in!
He is standing at the door.
Joy to you He will restore.
And His name you will adore:
Let Him in!

"Now admit the heavenly Guest.
Let Him in!

He will make for you a feast:
Let Him in!
He will speak your sins forgiven,
And when earth-ties all are riven,
He will take you home to heaven,
Let Him in!"

> Rev. F. B. Atckinson

# 5

## LAW AND GRACE

In his epistle to the Romans, Paul writes, "For as by one man's disobedience many were made sinners, so by the obedience of one shall many be made righteous. Moreover the law entered, that the offence might abound. But where sin abounded, grace did much more abound: that as sin hath reigned unto death, even so might grace reign through righteousness unto eternal life by Jesus Christ our Lord" (5:19–21).

Moses was the representative of the law. You remember that he led the children of Israel through the wilderness and brought them to Jordan, but there he left them. He could take them up to the river, which is a type of death and judgment; but Joshua (which means Jesus—Savior) led them right through death and judgment—through the Jordan into the Promised Land. Here we have the difference between law and grace; between the law and the Gospel.

Take another illustration. John the Baptist was the last prophet of the old dispensation—the last prophet under the law. You remember

that before Christ made His appearance at the
Jordan, the cry of John day by day was, "Repent:
for the kingdom of God is at hand!" He thun-
dered out the law. He took his hearers down to
the Jordan and baptized them. He put them in
the place of death; and that was as far as he
could take them. But there was One coming after him who could take them into the Promised
Land. As Joshua led the people through the
Jordan into Canaan—so Christ went down into
the Jordan of death, through death and judgment, on to resurrection ground.

If you run all through Scripture, you will
find that the law brings us to death. "Sin hath
reigned unto death" (Romans 5:21). A friend
was telling me lately that an acquaintance of
his, a minister, was once called upon to offici-
ate at a funeral, in the place of a chaplain of
one of Her Majesty's prisons, who was absent.
He noticed that only one solitary man followed
the body of the criminal to the grave. When
the grave had been covered, this man told the
minister that he was an officer of the law whose
duty it was to watch the body of the culprit
until it was buried out of sight; that was "the
end" of the British law.

And that is what the law of God does to the
sinner: it brings him right to death, and leaves
him there. I pity deep down in my heart those
who are trying to save themselves by the law. It
never has, it never will, and it never can—save

the soul. When people say they are going to try and do their best, and so save themselves by the law, I like to take them on their own ground. Have they ever done their very best? Granting that there *might* be a chance for them if they had, was there ever a time when they could not have done a little better? If a man wants to do his best, let him accept the grace of God; that is the best thing that any man or woman can possibly do.

But you will ask, What is the law given for? It may sound rather strange, but it is given that it may stop every man's mouth. "We know that what things soever the law saith, it saith to them who are under the law: that every mouth may be stopped, and all the world may become guilty before God. Therefore by the deeds of the law there shall no flesh be justified in his sight: for by the law is the knowledge of sin." The law shuts my mouth; grace opens it. The law locks up my heart; grace opens it—and then the fountain of love begins to flow out. When men get their eyes opened to see this glorious truth, they will cease their constant struggle. They will give up trying to work their way into the kingdom of God by the deeds of the law. They will give themselves up for lost, and take salvation as a free gift.

Life never came through the law. As someone has observed, when the law was given, three thousand men lost life; but when grace and truth came at Pentecost, three thousand obtained life. Under the law, if a man became a drunkard, the magistrates would take him out and stone him to death. When the prodigal came home, grace met him and embraced him. Law says, Stone him!—grace says, Embrace him! Law says, Smite him!—grace says, Kiss him! Law went after him, and bound him; grace said, Loose him and let him go! Law tells me how crooked I am; grace comes and makes me straight.

I pity those who are always hanging around Sinai, hoping to get life there. I have an old friend in Chicago who is always lingering at Sinai. He is a very good man; but I think he will have a different story to tell when he gets home to heaven. He thinks I preach free grace too much; and I must confess I do like to speak of the free grace of God. This friend of mine feels as though he has a kind of mission to follow me; and whenever he gets a chance he comes in with the thunders of Sinai. I never yet met him but he was thundering away from Horeb. The last time I was in Chicago, I said to him, "Are you still lingering around Sinai?" "Yes," said he, "I believe in the law." I have made inquiries, and I never heard of anyone being converted under his preaching; the effects have always dwindled and died out. If the law is the door to heaven, there is no hope for any of us. A perfect God can only have a perfect standard. He that offends in one point is guilty of all; so "all have sinned, and come short of the glory of God."

Paul says to the Galatians: "Is the law then against the promises of God? God forbid: for if there had been a law given which could have given life, verily righteousness should have been by the law. But the scripture hath concluded all under sin, that the promise by faith of Jesus Christ might be given to them that believe. But before faith came, we were kept under the law, shut up unto the faith which should afterwards be revealed. Wherefore the law was our schoolmaster to bring us unto Christ, that we might be justified by faith. But after that faith is come, we are no longer under a schoolmaster. For ye are all the children of God by faith in Christ Jesus" (3:21–26).

## The Softening Power of Grace

So we see that the law cannot give life; all it can do is to bring us to Him who is the life. The law is said to be "a schoolmaster." Perhaps some of you do not know what a schoolmaster is. If you had been under the same schoolmaster as I was when a boy, you would have known. He had a good cane and it was frequently in use. In the little country district where I went to school, there were two parties; for the sake of illustration we may call the one the "law" party and the other the "grace" party. The law party said that boys could not possibly be controlled without the cane; and they kept a schoolmaster there who acted on their plan. The struggle went on, and at last, on one election day, the law party was put out, and the grace party ruled in their stead. I happened to be at the school that time; and I remember we said to each other that we were going to have a grand time that winter. There would be no more corporeal punishment, and we were going to be ruled by love.

I was one of the first to break the rules of the school. We had a lady teacher, and she asked me to stay behind. I thought the cane was coming out again; and I was going to protest against it. I was quite in a fighting mood. She took me alone. She sat down and began to talk to me kindly. I thought that was worse than the cane; I did not like it. I saw that she had not got any cane. She said: "I have made up my mind that if I cannot control the school by love, I will give it up. I will have no punishment; and if you love me, try and keep the rules of the school." I felt something right here in my throat. I was not one to shed many tears; but they would come—I could not keep them back. I said to her, "You will have no more trouble with me"; and she did not. I learned more that winter than in the other three put together.

That was the difference between law and

grace. Christ says, "If you love me, keep my commandments" (John 14:15). He takes us out from under the law, and puts us under grace. Grace will break the hardest heart. It was the love of God that prompted Him to send His only begotten Son into the world that He might save it. I suppose the thief had gone through his trial unsoftened. Probably the law had hardened his heart. But on the cross no doubt that touching prayer of the Savior, "Father, forgive them!" broke his heart, so that he cried, "Lord, remember me!" He was brought to ask for mercy. I believe there is no man so far gone but the grace of God will melt his heart.

It is told of Isaac T. Hopper, the Quaker, that he once encountered a profane colored man, named Cain, in Philadelphia, and took him before a magistrate, who fined him for blasphemy. Twenty years after, Hopper met Cain, whose appearance was much changed for the worse. This touched the Friend's heart. He stepped up, spoke kindly, and shook hands with the forlorn being. "Dost thou remember me," said the Quaker, "how I had thee fined for swearing?"

"Yes, indeed, I do: I remember what I paid as well as if it was yesterday."

"Well, did it do thee any good?"

"No, never a bit; it made me mad to have my money taken from me."

Hopper invited Cain to reckon up the interest on the fine, and paid him principal and interest too. "I meant it for thy good, Cain; and I am sorry I did thee any harm."

Cain's countenance changed; the tears rolled down his cheeks. He took the money with many thanks, became a quiet man, and was not heard to swear again.

### Peace, Grace, and Glory

So there is a great deal of difference between law and grace. "Being justified by faith, we have peace with God through our Lord Jesus Christ: by whom also we have access by faith into this grace wherein we stand, and rejoice in hope of the glory of God" (Romans 5:1–2). There are three precious things here: peace for the past; grace for the present; and glory for the future. There is no *peace* until we see the finished work of Jesus Christ—until we can look back and see the cross of Christ between us and our sins. When we see that Jesus was "the end of the law for righteousness" (Romans 10:4); that He "taste[d] death for every man" (Hebrews 2:9); that He "suffered . . . the just for the unjust" (1 Peter 3:18)—then comes peace. Then there is "the *grace* wherein we now stand." There is plenty of grace for us as we need it—day by day, and hour by hour.

Then there is *glory* for the time to come. A great many people seem to forget that the best is before us. Dr. Bonar says that everything before the true believer is "glorious." This thought took hold of my soul; and I began to look the matter up, and see what I could find in Scripture that was glorious hereafter. I found that the kingdom we are going to inherit is glorious; our crown is to be a "crown of glory"; the city we are going to inhabit is the city of the glorified; the songs we are to sing are the songs of the glorified; we are to wear garments of "glory and beauty"; our society will be the society of the glorified; our rest is to be "glorious"; the country to which we are going is to be full of "the glory of God and of the Lamb." There are many who are always looking on the backward path, and mourning over the troubles through which they have passed. They keep lugging up the cares and anxieties they have been called on to bear, and are forever looking at them. Why should we go reeling and staggering under the burdens and cares of life when we have such prospects before us?

If there is nothing but glory beyond, our faces ought to shine brightly all the time. If a skeptic were to come up here and watch the countenances of the audience he would find many of you looking as though there was anything but glory before you. Many a time it seems to me as if I were at a funeral, people look so sad and downcast. They do not appear to know much of the joy of the Lord. Surely if we were looking right on to the glory that awaits us, our faces would be continually lit up with the light of the upper world. We can preach by our countenances if we will.

The nearer we draw to that glory-land, where we shall be with Christ—the more peace, and joy, and rest we ought to have. If we will but come to the throne of grace, we shall have strength to bear all our troubles and trials. If you were to take all the afflictions that flesh is heir to and put them right on any one of us, God has grace enough to carry us right through without faltering.

Someone has compiled the following, which beautifully describes the contrast between law and grace:

THE LAW was given by Moses.

GRACE and truth came by Jesus Christ.

THE LAW says—This do, and thou shalt live.

GRACE says—Live, and then thou shalt do.

THE LAW says—Pay me what thou owest.

GRACE says—I frankly forgive thee all.

THE LAW says—The wages of sin is death.

GRACE says—The gift of God is eternal life.

THE LAW says—The soul that sinneth, it shall die.

GRACE says—Whosoever believeth in Jesus, though he were dead, yet shall he live;

and whosoever liveth and believeth in Him shall never die.

THE LAW pronounces—Condemnation and death.

GRACE proclaims—Justification and life.

THE LAW says—Make you a new heart and a new spirit.

GRACE says—A new heart will I give you, and a new spirit will I put within you.

THE LAW says—Cursed is every one that continueth not in all things which are written in the book of the law to do them.

GRACE says—Blessed is the man whose iniquities are forgiven, whose sin is covered; blessed is the man to whom the Lord will not impute iniquity.

THE LAW says—Thou shalt love the Lord thy God with all thy heart, and with all thy mind, and with all thy strength.

GRACE says—Herein is love; not that we love God, but that He loved us, and sent His Son to be the propitiation for our sins.

THE LAW speaks of what man must do for God.

GRACE tells of what Christ has done for man.

THE LAW addresses man as part of the old creation.

GRACE makes a man a member of the new creation.

THE LAW bears on a nature prone to disobedience.

GRACE creates a nature inclined to obedience.

THE LAW demands obedience by the terror of the Lord.

GRACE beseeches men by the mercies of God.

THE LAW demands holiness.

GRACE gives holiness.

THE LAW says—Condemn him.

GRACE says—Embrace him.

THE LAW speaks of priestly sacrifices offered year by year continually, which could never make the comers thereunto perfect.

GRACE says—But this Man, after he had offered one sacrifice for sins forever . . . by one offering hath perfected forever them that are sanctified.

THE LAW declares—That as many as have sinned in the Law, shall be judged by the Law.

GRACE brings eternal peace to the troubled soul of every child of God, and proclaims God's salvation in defiance of the accusations of the adversary. "He that heareth my word, and believeth on him that sent me, hath everlasting life, and shall not come into condemnation, but is passed from death unto life."

# 6
## GRACE FOR LIVING

Now we come to a very important part of our subject: grace for living. One of the saddest things in the present day is the fact that so many professed Christians have no spiritual power. They bear no testimony for Christ. There are so few who can go to the homes of the sick and read the Bible to them, pray with them, and minister comfort to their souls. How few can go to the abode of the drunkard, and tell him of Christ's power to save! How few there are who are wise in winning souls to Christ!

It is the low spiritual state of so many in the church of Christ that is the trouble. We are not living up to our privileges. As you go through the streets of London you will see here and there the words, "Limited Company." There are many Christians who practically limit the grace of God. It is like a river flowing by; and we can have all we need: but if we do not come and get a continual supply, we cannot give it out to others.

Mother! Father! Are you not longing to see your children won to Christ? What is the trou-

ble? Is it the fault of the minister? I believe that
though ministers were to preach like angels, if
there is a low standard of Christian life in the
home, there will be little accomplished. What
we want, more than anything else, is more
grace in our lives, in our business affairs, in our
homes, in our daily walk and conversation. I
cannot but believe that the reason of the standard of Christian life being so low is that we are
living on stale manna. You know what I mean
by that. So many people are living on their past
experience—thinking of the grand times they
had twenty years ago, perhaps when they were
converted. It is a sure sign that we are out of
communion with God if we are talking more of
the joy and peace and power we had in the past
than of what we have today. We are told to
"grow in grace"; but a great many are growing
the wrong way.

You remember the Israelites used to gather
the manna fresh every day; they were not
allowed to store it up. There is a lesson here for
us Christians. If we would be strong and vigor-
ous, we must go to God daily and get grace. A
man can no more take in a supply of grace for
the future than he can eat enough today to last
him for the next six months; or take sufficient
air into his lungs at once to sustain life for a
week to come. We must draw upon God's
boundless stores of grace from day to day, as we
need it.

I knew a man who lived on the banks of Lake Erie. He had pipes laid to his house from the lake; and when he wanted water, all he had to do was to turn the tap and the water flowed in. If the government had presented him with the lake, he would not have known what to do with it. So we may say that if God were to give us grace enough for a lifetime, we should not know how to use it. He has given us the privilege of drawing on Him day by day—not "forty days after sight." There is plenty of grace in the bank of heaven; we need not be afraid of its becoming exhausted.

We are asked to come *boldly* to the throne of grace as sons to a father—that we may find grace. You have noticed that a son is very much more bold in his father's house than if he were simply a servant. A good many Christians are like servants. If you go into a house, you can soon tell the difference between the family and the servants. A son comes home in the evening; he goes all over the house—perhaps talks about the letters that have come in, and wants to know all that has been going on in the family during his absence. It is very different with a servant, who perhaps does not leave the kitchen or the servants' hall all day except when duty requires it.

Suppose someone had paid a million dollars into the bank in your name, and had given you a checkbook so that you could draw out just as you wanted: would you go to work and try to live on ten dollars a month? Yet that is exactly what many of us are doing as Christians. I believe this low standard of Christian life in the church is doing more to manufacture infidels than all the skeptical books that were ever written.

Hear what the apostle says: "My God shall supply *all* your need" (Philippians 4:19, italics added). Look at these words carefully. It does not say He will supply all your *wants*. There are many things we want that God has not promised to give. It is "your *need*" and "*all* your need." My children often want many things that they do not get; but I supply all they need, if it is in my power to give it to them. I do not supply all their wants by any means. My boy would probably want to have me give him a horse, when I know that what he really needs, perhaps, is grace to control his temper.

Our children might want many things that it would be injurious for them to have. And so, though God may withhold from us many things that we desire, He will supply all our need. There can come upon us no trouble or trial in this life, but God has grace enough to carry us right through it, if we will only go to Him and get it. But we must ask for it day by day. "As thy days, so shall thy strength be."

I met a man once in Scotland who taught me a lesson that I shall never forget. A Christian friend wanted me to go and have a talk with him. He had been bedridden for many years. This afflicted saint comforted me and told me some wonderful things. He had fallen and broken his back when he was about fifteen years of age, and had lain there on his bed for some forty years. He could not be moved without a good deal of pain, and probably not a day had passed all those years without suffering. If anyone had told him he was going to lie there and suffer for forty years, probably he would have said he could not do it. But day after day the grace of God has been granted to him; and I declare to you it seemed to me as if I were in the presence of one of God's most highly favored children.

It seemed that when I was in that man's chamber, I was about as near heaven as I could get on this earth. Talk about a man's face shining with the glory of the upper world! I very seldom see a face that shines as did his. I can imagine that the very angels when they are passing over the city on some mission of mercy, come down into that man's chamber to get refreshed. There he has been lying all these years, not only without a murmur, but rejoicing all the while.

I said to him: "My friend, does the devil never tempt you to doubt God, and to think He is a hard master?"

"Well now," he said, "that is just what he

tries to do. Sometimes, as I look out of the window and see people walking along in health, Satan whispers: 'If God is so good, why does He keep you here all these weary years? Why, if He loved you, instead of lying here and being dependent on others, you might now have been a rich man, and riding in your own carriage.'"

"What do you do when the devil tempts you?"

"Oh, I just take him up to the Cross; and he had such a fright there eighteen hundred years ago, that he cannot stand it; and he leaves me."

I do not think that bedridden saint has much trouble with doubts; he is so full of grace.

And so if we will only come boldly to God, we shall get all the help and strength we need. There is not a man or woman alive but may be kept from falling, if they will let God hold them up in His almighty arms.

There is a story in the history of Elisha the prophet that I am very fond of; most of you are familiar with it. Sometimes we meet with people who hesitate to accept Christ, because they are so afraid they will not hold out. You remember there was a young prophet who died and left a widow with two little boys. It has been said that misfortunes do not come singly, but in battalions. This woman had not only lost her husband, but a creditor was going to take her boys and sell them into slavery. That was a common thing in those days. The widow went and told Elisha all about it. He asked her what she had in the house. Nothing, she said, but a pot of oil. It was a very hard case.

Elisha told her to go home and borrow all the vessels she could. His command was: "Borrow not a few." I like that. She took him at his word and borrowed all the vessels her neighbors would lend to her. I can imagine the woman and her two sons going from house to house asking the loan of their vessels. No doubt there were a good many of the neighbors who were stretching their necks and wondering what it all meant, just as we sometimes find people coming into the inquiry-room to see what is going on. If this woman had been like some modern skeptics, she would have thought it very absurd for the prophet to bid her do such a thing; she would have asked what good could come of it. But faith asks no questions; so she went and did what the man of God told her to do. I can see her going up one side of the street knocking at every door and asking for empty vessels. "How many do you want?" "All you can spare."

There were the two sons carrying the great vessels, some of them perhaps nearly as large as the boys themselves. It was hard work. When they had finished one side of the street, they went down the other. "Borrow not a few," she

had been told; so she went on asking for as
many as she could get. If there were as much
gossip in those days as there is now, all the people in the street would have been talking about
her. "Why, this woman and her boys have been
carrying vessels into the house all day; what can
be the matter?"

But now they had all the vessels the neighbors would lend. She locked the door and said
to one of the boys, "James, you are the younger;
bring me the empty vessels. John, you are the
stronger; when I have filled them, you take
them away." So she began to pour. Perhaps the
first vessel was twice as big as the one she
poured from; but it was soon filled, and she
kept on pouring into vessel after vessel. At last
her son says, "Mother, this is the last one"; and
we are told that the oil was not stayed till the
last vessel was full.

Dear friends, bring your empty vessels and
God will fill them. I venture to say that the eyes
of those boys sparkled as they saw this beautiful
oil, fresh from the land of the Creator. The
woman went and told the man of God what
had happened. He said to her, "Go, sell the oil,
and pay thy debt; and live thou and thy children of the rest." That is grace for the present
and for the future. "As thy days, so shall thy
strength be" (Deuteronomy 33:25). You will
have grace not only to cover all your sins, but to
carry you right into glory. Let the grace of God

into your heart; and He will bring you safely through.

Let me close by quoting the words of an old prayer: "God give us grace to see our need of grace; give us grace to ask for grace; give us grace to receive grace; give us grace to use the grace we have received."

"Grace taught my soul to pray,
And pardoning love to know;
'Twas grace that kept me to this day,
And will not let me go.

"Grace all the work shall crown,
Through everlasting days;
It lays in heaven the topmost stone,
And well deserves the praise!"

# 7

## GRACE FOR SERVICE

"For the grace of God that bringeth salvation hath appeared to all men, teaching us that, denying ungodliness and worldly lusts, we should live soberly, righteously, and godly, in this present world; looking for that blessed hope, and the glorious appearing of the great God and our Saviour Jesus Christ; who gave himself for us, that he might redeem us from all iniquity, and purify unto himself a peculiar people, zealous of good works" (Titus 2:11–13).

In this wonderful passage we see grace in a threefold aspect: grace that bringeth salvation; grace for holy living; and grace for service. I have had three red-letter days in my experience: the first was when I was converted; the next was when I got my lips opened, and I began to confess Christ; the third was when I began to work for the salvation of others.

I think there are a great many who have got to the first stage; some have got to the second; very few have got to the third. This is the reason, I believe, why the world is not reached.

Many say they are anxious to "grow in grace." I do not think they ever will until they

go out into the harvest field and begin to work
for others. We are not going to have the grace
we need to qualify us for work until we launch
out into the deep and begin to use the abilities
and the opportunities we already possess. Many
fold their arms and wait for the grace of God to
come to them: but we do not get it in that way.
When we "go forward," then it is that God
meets us with His grace.

If Moses had stayed in Horeb until he got
the grace he needed, he never would have
started for Egypt at all. But when he had set
out, God met him in the way and blessed him
day by day as he needed. Many grow discouraged because there is a little opposition; but if
we are going to work for God we must expect
opposition. No real work was ever done for
God without opposition. If you think that you
are going to have the approval of a godless
world and of cold Christians as you launch out
into the deep with your net, you are greatly
mistaken. A man said to me some time ago that
when he was converted he commenced to do
some work in connection with the church; he
was greatly discouraged because some of the
older Christians threw cold water on him, so he
gave up the whole thing.

I pity a man who cannot take a little cold
water without being any the worse for it. Why,
many of the Christians in old times had to go

through the fire, and did not shrink from it. A little cold water never hurts anyone.

Others say they have so many cares and troubles, they have as much as they can carry. Well, a good way to forget your trouble is to go and help someone else who is carrying a heavier burden than yourself. It was when Job began to pray for his friends that he forgot his own troubles. Paul gloried in his infirmity and in the tribulations he had to undergo, so that the power of Christ might all the more rest upon him. He gloried in the Cross, and you must bear in mind that the Cross was not so easy to bear in his day as it is in ours. Everyone was speaking against it. "I glory in the Cross of Christ," he said. When a man gets to that point, do you tell me that God cannot use him to build up His kingdom? In his second letter to the Corinthians, Paul speaks of "the thorn in the flesh" (12:7); he prayed the Lord to take it away. The Lord said He was not going to take it away, but He would give His servant grace to bear it. So the apostle learned to thank God for the thorn, because he got more grace. It is when the days are dark that people are brought nearer to God. I suppose that is what Paul meant.

If there is any child of God who has a "thorn in the flesh," God has grace enough to help you to bear it if you will but go to Him for it. The difficulty is that so many are looking at their troubles and sorrows, instead of looking toward the glorious reward, and pressing on their way by God's help.

In 2 Corinthians 9:8, we read: "God is able to make all grace abound toward you; that ye, always having all sufficiency in all things, may abound to every good work." There are three thoughts here—God makes *all grace* to abound, that we may have *all sufficiency* in *all things*. I think this is one of the most wonderful verses in the Bible.

There is plenty of grace. Many Christians, if they have grace enough to keep them from outward sin, seem to be perfectly satisfied; they do not press on to *get fullness of grace,* so as to be ready for God's work. Many are satisfied to go into the stream of grace ankle deep, when God wants them to swim in it.

If we always came to meetings desiring to get strength, then we should be able to go out to work and speak for Christ. There are a great many who would be used of God, if they would only come boldly to His throne of grace, and "find grace to help in time of need." Is it not a time of need now? God has said, "I will pour water on him that is thirsty." Do we thirst for a deeper work of grace in our hearts?—for the anointing of the Spirit? Here is the promise: "I will pour water on him that is thirsty" (Isaiah 44:3). Let all who are hungering and thirsting for blessing come and receive it.

Another reason why many Christians do not get anything is because they do not give out to others. They are satisfied with present attainments, instead of growing in grace. We are not the fountain; we are only a channel for the grace of God to flow through. There is not one of us but God wants to use in building up His kingdom. That little boy, that gray-haired man, these young men and maidens; all are needed: and there is a work for all. We want to believe that God has grace enough to qualify us to go out and work for Him.

If we have known Jesus Christ for twenty years or more, and if we have not been able to introduce an anxious soul to Him, there has been something wrong somewhere. If we were full of grace, we should be ready for any call that comes to us. Paul said, when he had that famous interview with Christ on the way to Damascus, "Lord, what wilt thou have me to do?" Isaiah said, "Here am I send me." Oh, that God would fill all His people with grace, so that we may see more wonderful things than He has ever permitted us to see! No man can tell what he can do, until he moves forward. If we do that in the name of God, instead of there being a few scores or hundreds converted, there will be thousands flocking into the kingdom of God. Remember that we honor God when we ask for great things. It is a humiliating thing to think that we are satisfied with very small results.

It is said that Alexander the Great had a favorite general to whom he had given permission to draw upon the royal treasury for any amount. On one occasion this general had made a draft for such an enormous sum that the treasurer refused to honor it until he consulted the emperor. So he went into his presence and told him what the general had done. "Did you not honor the draft?" said the emperor. "No; I refused till I had seen your Majesty; because the amount was so great." The emperor was indignant. His treasurer said that he was afraid of offending him if he had paid the amount. "Do you not know," replied the emperor, "that he honors me and my kingdom by making a large draft?" Whether the story be authentic or not, it is true that we honor God when we ask for great things.

It is said that on one occasion when Caesar gave a very valuable present, the receiver replied that it was too costly a gift. The emperor answered that it was not too great for Caesar to give. Our God is a great king and He delights to use us; so let us delight to ask Him for great grace, that we may go out and work for Him.

I find that many Christians are in trouble about the future; they think they will not have grace enough to die by. It is much more important that we should have grace enough to live by. It seems to me that death is of very little importance in the meantime. When the dying hour comes there will be dying grace; but you do not require dying grace to live by. If I am going to live perhaps for fifteen or twenty years, what do I want with dying grace? I am far more anxious about having grace enough for my present work.

I have sometimes been asked if I had grace enough to enable me to go to the stake and die as a martyr. No; what do I want with martyrs' grace? I do not like suffering; but if God should call on me to die a martyr's death, He would give me martyrs' grace. If I have to pass through some great affliction, I know God will give me grace when the time comes; but I do not want it till it comes.

There is a story of a martyr in the second century. He was brought before the king, and told that if he did not recant they would banish him. Said he, "O king, you cannot banish me from Christ; for He has said, "I will never leave thee nor forsake thee!" The apostle John was banished to the island of Patmos, but it was the best thing that could have happened; for if John had not been sent there, probably we should never have had that grand book of Revelation. John could not be separated from his Master.

So it was with this brave martyr, of whom I was speaking. The king said to him, "Then I will take away your property from you."

"You cannot do that, for my treasure is laid up on high, where you cannot get at it."

"Then I will kill you."

"You cannot do that; for I have been dead these forty years: 'my life is hid with Christ in God.'"

The king said, "What are you going to do with such a fanatic as that?"

Let us remember that if we have not grace enough for service, we have no one to blame but ourselves. We are not straitened in God; He has abundance of grace to qualify us to work for Him.

### More to Follow

I heard a story about two members of a church: one was a wealthy man, and the other was one of those who could not take care of his finances—he was always in debt. The rich brother had compassion on his poor brother. He wanted to give him some money, but he would not give it to the man all at once: he knew he would not use it properly. So he sent the amount to the minister, and asked him to supply the needs of this poor brother. The minister used to send him a five-dollar bill, and put on the envelope "More to follow." I can imagine how welcome the gift would be; but the best of all was the promise: "More to follow." So it is with God: there is always "more to follow."

It is such a pity that we are not ready to be used by God when He wants to use us.

Dear friends, let me put this question to you: Are you full of grace? You shake your head. Well, it is our privilege to be full. What is the best way to get full of grace? It is to be emptied of self. How can we be emptied? Suppose you wish to get the air out of this tumbler; how can you do it? I will tell you: by pouring water into the tumbler till it is full to overflowing. That is the way the Lord empties us of self. He fills us with His grace. "I will pour water on him that is thirsty." Are you hungering to get rid of your sinful selves? Then let the Spirit of God come in and fill you. God is able to do it.

See what He did for John Bunyan—how He made one of the mightiest instruments for good the world ever saw out of that swearing Bedford tinker. If we had a telescope which would enable us to look into heaven as Stephen did, I can imagine we should see the thief, who believed in Jesus while on the cross, very near the throne. Ask him how he got there, and he would tell you it was through the grace of God. See how the grace of God could save a Mary Magdalene possessed of seven devils! Ask her what it was that melted her heart, and she would tell you that it was the grace of God. Look again at that woman whom Christ met at the well at Sychar. The Savior offered her a cup of the living water. She drank, and now she walks the crystal pavement of heaven. See how the grace of God could change Zaccheus, the hated publican of Jericho! Now he is in yonder world of light; he was brought there by the sovereign grace of God.

You will have noticed that many of those who were about the most unlikely have, by the power of God's grace, become very eminent in His service. Look at the twelve apostles of Christ; they were all unlettered men. This ought to encourage all whose education is limited to give themselves to God's work. When our earthly work is ended, then, like our Master, we shall enter into glory. It has been well remarked, "Grace is glory militant; and glory is grace triumphant. Grace is glory begun; glory is grace made perfect. Grace is the first degree of glory; glory is the highest degree of grace."

> Oh, to grace how great a debtor
> Daily I'm constrained to be!
> Let Thy grace, Lord, like a fetter,
> Bind my wandering heart to thee.
> Prone to wander, Lord, I feel it—
> Prone to leave the God I love—
> Here's my heart, oh take and seal it,
> Seal it for Thy courts above.

# 8

## A CHIME OF GOSPEL BELLS

In Baltimore a few years ago, we held a
number of meetings for men. I am very fond of
this hymn; and we used to let the choir sing the
chorus over and over again, till all could sing it.

Oh, word of words the sweetest,
Oh, word in which there lie
All promise, all fulfillment,
And end of mystery!
Lamenting or rejoicing,
With doubt or terror nigh,
I hear the "Come!" of Jesus,
And to His cross I fly.

Come! oh, come to me!
Come! oh, come to me!
Weary heavy-laden,
Come! oh, come to Me!

O soul! why shouldst thou wander
From such a loving Friend?
Cling closer, closer to Him
Stay with Him to the end
Alas! I am so helpless,
So very full of sin;

For I am ever wandering,
And coming back again.

Oh, each time draw me nearer,
That soon the "Come!" may be
Nought but a gentle whisper
To one close, close to Thee;
Then, over sea and mountain,
Far from, or near, my home,
I'll take Thy hand and follow,
At that sweet whisper, "Come!"

There was a man in one of the meetings who had been brought there against his will; he had come through some personal influence brought to bear upon him. When he got to the meeting, they were singing the chorus of this hymn: "Come! Come! Come!"

He said afterwards he thought he never saw so many fools together in his life before. The idea of a number of men standing there singing, "Come! Come! Come!" When he started home he could not get this little word out of his head; it kept coming back all the time. He went into a saloon and ordered some whiskey, thinking to drown it. But he could not; it still kept coming back. He went into another saloon, and drank some more whiskey; but the words kept ringing in his ears: "Come! Come! Come!" He said to himself, "What a fool I am for allowing myself to be troubled in this way!"

He went to a third saloon, had another glass, and finally got home.

He went off to bed, but could not sleep; it seemed as if the very pillow kept whispering the words, "Come! Come!" He began to be angry with himself: "What a fool I was for ever going to that meeting at all." When he got up he took the little hymnbook, found the hymn, and read it over. "What nonsense!" he said to himself. "The idea of a rational man being disturbed by that hymn." He set fire to the hymnbook; but he could not burn up the little word "Come!" "Heaven and earth shall pass away: but my word shall not pass away."

He declared he would never go to another of the meetings; but the next night he came again. When he got there, strange to say, they were singing the same hymn. "There is that miserable old hymn again," he said; "what a fool I am for coming!" I tell you, when the Spirit of God lays hold of a man, he does a good many things he did not intend to do. To make a long story short, that man rose in a meeting of young converts and told the story that I have now told you. Pulling out the little hymnbook—for he had bought another copy—and opening it at this hymn, he said, "I think this hymn is the sweetest and the best in the English language. God blessed it to the saving of my soul." And yet this was the very hymn he had despised.

I want to take up this little word "Come!" Sometimes people forget the text of a sermon, but this text will be short enough for anyone to remember. Let me ring out a chime of Gospel bells, every one of which says, "Come!"

The first bell I will ring is:

## Come and Hear!

"Incline your ear, and *come* unto me: *hear,* and your soul shall live; and I will make an everlasting covenant with you, even the sure mercies of David" (Isaiah 55:3).

"Incline your ear," God says. You have sometimes seen a man who is a little deaf, and cannot catch every word, put his hand up to his ear and lean forward. I have seen a man sometimes put up both hands to his ears, as if he were determined to catch every word. I like to see that. This is the figure that the prophet uses when he says on God's behalf, "Incline your ear."

Man lost spiritual life and communion with his Maker by listening to the voice of the tempter, instead of the voice of God. We get life again by listening to the voice of God. The Word of God gives life. "The words that I speak unto you," says Christ, "they are spirit, and they are life" (John 6:63). So, what people need is to incline their ear and *hear*. It is a great thing when the Gospel preacher gets the ear of a congregation—I mean the inner ear. For a man has not only two ears in his head; he has also what we may call the inner ear—the ear of the soul. You may speak to the outward ear, and not reach the ear of the soul at all.

Many in these days are like the "foolish people" to whom the prophet Jeremiah spoke: "Which have eyes, and see not; which have ears, and hear not" (Jeremiah 5:21). There are many in every congregation whose attention I am not able to secure for five minutes together. Almost any little thing will divert their minds. We need to give heed to the words of the Lord: "He that hath ears to hear, let him hear."

When Peter was sent to Cornelius, he was to speak to him words whereby he and his house were to be saved. If you are to be saved, it must be by listening to the Word of God. Here is the promise: "Hear; and your soul shall live" (Isaiah 55:3).

There was an architect in Chicago who was converted. In giving his testimony, he said he had been in the habit of attending church for a great many years, but he could not say that he had really heard a sermon all the time. He said that when the minister gave out the text and began to preach, he used to settle himself in the corner of the pew and work out the plans of some building. He could not tell how many plans he had prepared while the minister was preaching. He was the architect for one or two companies; and he used to do all his planning in that way. You see, Satan came in between him and the preacher, and caught away the good seed of the Word. I have often preached to people, and have been perfectly amazed to find they could hardly tell one solitary word of the sermon; even the text had completely gone from them.

A colored man once said that a good many of his congregation would be lost because they were too generous. He saw that the people looked rather surprised; so he said, "Perhaps you think I have made a mistake, and that I ought to have said you will be lost because you are not generous enough. That is not so; I meant just what I said. You give away too many sermons. You hear them, as it were, for other people." So there are a good many now hearing me who are listening for those behind them. They say the message is a very good one for neighbor So-and-so; and they pass it over their shoulders, till it gets clear out at the door. You laugh; but you know it is so. Listen! "Verily, verily, I say unto you, He that heareth my word, and believeth on him that sent me, hath everlasting life, and shall not come into condemnation; but is passed from death unto life" (John 5:24).

The next note in this peal of bells I wish to ring out is:

## Come and See!

Scripture not only uses the ear but the eye in illustrating the way of salvation. When a man both hears and sees a thing, he remembers it twice as long as if he only heard it. You remember what Philip said to Nathanael: "Philip findeth Nathanael, and saith unto him, We have found him, of whom Moses in the law, and the prophets, did write, Jesus of Nazareth, the son of Joseph. And Nathanael said unto him, Can there any good thing come out of Nazareth? Philip saith unto him, Come and see" (John 1:45–46).

Philip was a wise winner of souls. He brought his friend to Christ. Nathanael had one interview with the Son of God; he became His disciple and never left Him. If Philip had gone on discussing the matter with him, and had tried to prove that some good thing could come out of Nazareth, he might have never been a disciple at all.

After all, we do not gain much by discussion. Let objectors or inquirers only get one personal interview with the Son of God; that will scatter all their darkness, all their prejudice, and all their unbelief. The moment that Philip succeeded in getting Nathanael to Christ, the work was done.

So we say to you, "Come and see!" I thought, when I was converted, that my friends had been very unfaithful to me, because they had not told me about Christ. I thought I would have all my friends converted inside of twenty-four hours; and I was quite disappoint-

ed when they did not at once see Christ to be
the Lily of the Valley, and the Rose of Sharon,
and the Bright and Morning Star. I wondered
why it was. No doubt many of those who hear
me now have had that experience; you thought
when you saw Christ in all His beauty that you
could soon make your friends see Him in the
same light.

But we need to learn that God alone can do
it. If there is a skeptic now hearing me, I want
to say that one personal interview with the Son
of God will scatter all your infidelity and atheism. One night, in the inquiry-room, I met the
wife of an atheist who had been brought to
God at one of our meetings. She was converted
at the same time. She had brought two of her
daughters to the meeting, desiring that they
too should know Christ. I said to the mother:
"How is it with your skepticism now?" "Oh,"
said she, "it is all gone. When Christ gets into
the heart, atheism must go out. If a man will
only come and take one trustful loving look at
the Savior, there will be no desire to leave Him
again."

A gentleman was walking down the street
in Baltimore a few years ago. It was near Christmas, and many of the shop windows were filled
with Christmas presents, toys, etc. As this gentleman passed along he saw three little girls
standing before a shop window and he heard
two of them trying to describe to the third the

things that were in the window. It aroused his attention, and he wondered what it could mean. He went back and found that the middle one was blind. She had never been able to see, and her two sisters were endeavoring to tell her how the thing looked. The gentleman stood beside them for some time and listened. Later he said it was most interesting to hear them trying to describe the different articles to the blind child; they found it a difficult task.

As he told me, I said to myself, "That is just my position in trying to tell other men about Christ: I may talk about Him, and yet they see no beauty in Him that they should desire Him. But if they will only come to Him, He will open their eyes and reveal Himself to them in all His loveliness and grace."

Looking at it from the outside, there was not much beauty in the Tabernacle that Moses erected in the desert. It was covered on the outside with badgers' skins—and there was not much beauty in them. If you were to pass into the inside, then you would find out the beauty of the coverings. So the sinner sees no beauty in Christ till he comes to Him—then he can see it.

You have looked at the windows of a grand church erected at the cost of many thousands of dollars. From the outside they did not seem very beautiful but get inside, when the rays of the sun are striking upon the stained glass, and you begin to understand what others have told you of their magnificence. So it is when you have come into personal contact with Christ: you find Him to be the very Friend you need. Therefore we extend to all the sweet Gospel invitation, "Come and see."

Let me now ring out the third bell:

## Come and Drink!

"Ho, every one that thirsteth, come ye to the waters, and he that hath no money; come ye, buy, and eat; yea, come, buy wine and milk without money and without price" (Isaiah 55:1). If you will come and drink at this fountain, Christ says you shall never thirst again. He has promised to quench your thirst. "If any man thirst," He says, "let him come unto me, and drink" (John 7:37).

I thank God for those words: *"If any man."* That does not mean merely a select, few respectable people; it takes in all—every drunkard, every harlot, every thief, every self-righteous Pharisee.

"If any man *thirst.*" How this world is thirsting for something that will satisfy! What fills the places of amusement—the dance houses, the music halls, and the theaters, night after night? Men and women are thirsting for something they have not got. The moment a man turns his back upon God, he begins to thirst; and that thirst will never be quenched until he returns to "the fountain of living waters." As the prophet Jeremiah tells us, we have forsaken the fountain of living waters, and hewn out for ourselves cisterns, broken cisterns, that can hold no water. There is a thirst this world can never quench; the more we drink of its pleasures, the thirstier we become. We cry out for more and more; and we are all the while being dragged down lower and lower. But there is "a fountain opened to the house of David . . . for sin and for uncleanness." Let us press up to it, and drink and live.

I remember after one of the great battles in the Civil War we were coming down the Tennessee River with a company of wounded men. It was in the spring of the year, and the water was not clear. You know that the cry of a wounded man is: "Water! Water!" especially in a hot country. I remember taking a glass of the muddy water to one of these men. Although he was very thirsty, he only drank a little of it. He handed the glass back to me, and as he did so, he said. "Oh, for a draught of water from my father's well!" Are there any thirsty ones here? Come and drink of the fountain opened in Christ. Your longing will be satisfied, and you will never thirst again. It will be in you "a well of water springing up into everlasting life" (John 4:14).

Water rises to its own level; and as this water has come down from the throne of God, it will carry us back to the presence of God. Come, O ye thirsty ones, stoop down and drink, and live! You are all invited: come along!

When Moses took his rod and struck the flinty rock in the wilderness, out of it there came a pure crystal stream of water, which flowed on through that dry and barren land. All that the poor thirsty Israelites had to do was to stoop and drink; it was free to all. So the grace of God is free to all. God invites you to come and take it. Will you come?

I remember being in a large city where I noticed that the people resorted to a favorite well in one of the parks. I said to a man one day, "Does the well never run dry?" The man was drinking of the water out of the well; and as he stopped drinking, he smacked his lips, and said: "They have never been able to pump it dry yet. They tried it a few years ago. They put the fire engines to work, and tried all they could to pump the well dry; but they found there was a river flowing right under the city." Thank God, the well of salvation never gets dry, though the saints of God have been drinking from it for six thousand years! Abel, Enoch, Noah, Abraham, Moses, Elijah, the apostles—all have drunk from it and they are now up yonder, where they are drinking of the stream that flows from the throne of God. "They shall hunger no more, neither thirst any more; neither shall the sun light on them, nor any heat.

For the Lamb which is in the midst of the throne shall feed them, and shall lead them unto living fountains of waters: and God shall wipe away all tears from their eyes."

Let me ring another Gospel bell:

## Come and Dine!

My brother, my sister—are you hungry? Then come along and dine. Some people are afraid of being converted, because they think they will not hold out. Mr. Rainsford once said, "If the Lord gives us eternal life, He will surely give us all that is needful to preserve it." He not only gives life, but He gives us our daily bread to feed that life.

After the Savior had risen from the dead, He had not appeared to His disciples for some days. Peter said to the others, "I go a fishing." Seven of them started off in their boats. They toiled all night but caught nothing. In the gray of the morning, they saw a stranger on the shore. He addressed them and said, "Children, have ye any meat?" They told Him they had not. "Cast the net on the right side of the ship, and ye shall find."

I can imagine they said to each other, "What good is that going to do? We have been fishing here all night, and have got nothing. The idea that there should be fish on one side of the boat and not on the other!" However, they obeyed the command, and they had such a haul that there was no room for the fish in the boat. Then one of them said, "It is the Lord." When he heard that, Peter sprang right into the sea and swam to the shore, and the others pulled the boat to land.

When they reached the shore the Master said, "Come and dine." What a meal that must have been. There was the Lord of glory feeding His disciples. If He could set a table for His people in the wilderness, and feed three millions of Israelites for forty years, can He not give us our daily bread? I do not mean only the bread that perisheth; but the Bread that cometh from above. If He feeds the birds of the air, surely He will feed His children made in His own image! If He numbers the very hairs of our head, He will take care to supply all our temporal wants.

Not only so: He will give us the Bread of Life for the nourishment of the soul—the life that the world knows nothing of—if we will but go to Him. "I am that bread of Life," He says (John 7:48). As we feed on Him by faith, we get strength. Let our thoughts rest upon Him; and He will lift us above ourselves, and above the world, and satisfy our utmost desires.

Another Gospel bell is:

### Come and Rest!

Dear friend, do you not need rest? There is a restlessness all over the world today. Men are sighing and struggling after rest. The cry of the world is, "Where can rest be found?" The rich man that we read of in the parable pulled down his barns that he might build greater, and he said to his soul, "Take thine ease." He thought he was going to find rest in wealth; but he was disappointed. That night his soul was summoned away. No; there is no rest in wealth or pleasure.

Others think they will succeed in drowning their sorrows and troubles by indulging in drink; but that will only increase them. There is no peace, saith my God, to the wicked; they are like the troubled sea that cannot rest. We sometimes talk of the ocean as being as calm as a sea of glass; but it is never at rest; and here we have a faithful picture of the wicked man and woman.

Oh, weary soul, hear the sweet voice that comes ringing down through the ages: "Come unto me, all ye that labour and are heavy laden, and I will *give* you rest" (Matthew 11:28, italics added). Thank God, He does not *sell* it! If He did, some of us are so poor we could not buy; but we can all take a gift. That little boy there knows how to take a gift; that old man, living on borrowed time, and almost on the verge of another world, knows how to take a gift. The gift Jesus wants to bestow is rest: rest for time and rest for eternity. Every weary soul may have this rest if he will. But you must come to Christ and get it. Nowhere else can this rest be found. If you go to the world with your cares, your troubles, and your anxieties, all it can do is to put a few more on the top of them. The world is a poor place to go to for sympathy. As someone has said: "If you roll your burdens anywhere but on Christ, they will roll back on you with more weight than ever. Cast them on Christ; and He will carry them for you."

Here is another bell:

## Come and Reason!

Perhaps there are some infidels reading this. They are fond of saying to us, "Come and reason." But I want to draw their attention to the verses that go before this one in the first chapter of Isaiah. The trouble with a good many skeptics is this—they take a sentence here and there from Scripture without reference to the context. Let us see what this passage (Isaiah 1:15–18) says: "When ye spread forth your hands, I will hide mine eyes from you: yea, when ye make many prayers, I will not hear: your hands are full of blood. Wash you, make you clean; put away the evil of your doings from before mine eyes; cease to do evil; learn to do well; seek judgment, relieve the oppressed, judge the fatherless, plead for the widow."

*Then* we have the gracious invitation, "Come now, and let us reason together." Do you think

God is going to reason with a man whose hands are dripping with blood, and before he asks forgiveness and mercy? Will God reason with a man living in rebellion against Him? Nay. But if we turn from and confess our sin, then He will reason with us and pardon us. "Though your sins be as scarlet, they shall be as white as snow; though they be red like crimson, they shall be as wool."

But if a man persists in his rebellion against God, there is no invitation to him to come and reason and receive pardon. If I have been justly condemned to death by the law of the State, and am waiting the execution of my sentence, I am not in a position to reason with the governor. If he chooses to send me a free pardon, the first thing I have to do is to accept it; then he may allow me to come into his presence. But we must bear in mind that God is above our reason. When man fell, his reason became perverted; and he was not in a position to reason with God. "If any man will do his will, he shall know of the doctrine" (John 7:17).

We must be willing to forsake our sins. "Let the wicked forsake his way, and the unrighteous man his thoughts: and let him return unto the Lord, and He will have mercy upon him; and to our God, for he will abundantly pardon" (Isaiah 55:7). The moment a man is willing to part with his sins, God meets him in grace and offers him peace and pardon.

The next bell I would like to sound out is:

## Come to the Marriage!

"Behold, I have prepared my dinner: . . all things are ready: come unto the marriage" (Matthew 22:4). Who would not feel highly honored if they were invited to some fine residence, to the wedding of one of the members of the President's family? I can imagine you would feel rather proud of having received such an invitation. You would want all your friends to know it.

Probably you may never get such an invitation. But I have a far grander invitation for you here than that. I cannot speak for others; but if I know my own heart, I would rather be torn to pieces tonight, limb from limb, and die in the glorious hope of being at the marriage supper of the Lamb, than live in this world a thousand years and miss that appointment at the last. "Blessed are they which are called unto the marriage supper of the Lamb" (Revelation 19:9). It will be a fearful thing for any of us to see Abraham, Isaac, and Jacob taking their place in the kingdom of God, and be ourselves thrust out.

This is no myth, my friends; it is a real invitation. Every man and woman is invited. All things are now ready. The feast has been prepared at great expense. You may spurn the grace, and the gift of God; but you must bear in mind that it cost God a good deal before He could provide this feast. When He gave Christ He gave the richest jewel that heaven had. And now He sends out the invitation. He commands His servants to go into the highways, and hedges, and lanes, and compel them to come in, that His house may be full. Who will come?

You say you are not fit to come? If the President invited you to the White House, and the invitation said you were to come just as you were, and if the sentinel at the gate stopped you because you did not wear a dress suit, what would you do? Would you not show him the document signed in the name of the President? Then he would stand aside and let you pass. So, my friend, if you can prove to me that you are a sinner, I can prove to you that you are invited to this Gospel feast—to this marriage supper of the Lamb.

Let me ring out another bell in this Gospel chime:

### Come, Inherit the Kingdom!

"Then shall the King say unto them on his right hand, Come, ye blessed of my Father, inherit the kingdom prepared for you from the foundation of the world" (Matthew 25:34). A kingdom! Think of that! Think of a poor man in this world, struggling with poverty and want, invited to become possessor of a kingdom! It is no fiction. It is described as "an inheritance incorruptible, and undefiled, and that fadeth not away, reserved in heaven for you, who are kept by the power of God through faith unto salvation ready to be revealed in the last time." We are called to be kings and priests: that is a high calling. Surely no one who hears me intends to miss that kingdom! Christ said, "Seek ye first the kingdom of God." Those who inherit it shall go no more out. Yet another bell:

## Come Up Hither!

In the Revelation we find that the two witnesses were called up to heaven when their testimony was ended. So if we are faithful in the service of our king, we shall by and by hear a voice saying, "Come up hither!" There is going to be a separation one day. The man who has been persecuting his godly wife will some day find her missing. That drunkard who beats his children because they have been taught the way into the kingdom of God will miss them some day. They will be taken up out of the darkness and away from the persecution, up into the presence of God. When the voice of God saying, "Come up hither," is heard, calling His children home, there will be a grand jubilee. That glorious day will soon dawn. "Lift up your heads; for your redemption draweth nigh."

One more bell to complete the chime:

### Whosoever Will, Let Him Come!

It is the last time that the word "Come" appears in the Bible; and it occurs there over one thousand nine hundred times. We find it way back in Genesis, "Come thou and all thy house into the ark"; and it goes right along through Scripture. Prophets, apostles, and preachers have been ringing it out all through the ages. Now the record is about to be closed, and Christ tells John to put in one more invitation. After the Lord had been in glory for about sixty years, perhaps He saw some poor man stumbling over one of the apostles' letters about the doctrine of election. So He came to John in Patmos, and John was in the Spirit on the Lord's Day.

Christ said to His disciple, "Write these things to the churches." I can imagine John's pen moved very easily and very swiftly that day, for the hand of his Lord was upon him. The Master said to him, "Before you close up the Book, put in one more invitation; and make it so broad that the whole world shall know they are included, and not a single one may feel that he is left out." John began to write: "The Spirit and the bride say, Come," that is, the Spirit and the church; "and let him that heareth say, Come!"

If you have heard and received the message

yourself, pass it on to those near you; your religion is not a very real thing if it does not affect someone else. We have to get rid of this idea that the world is going to be reached by ministers alone. All those who have drunk of the cup of salvation must pass it around.

"Let him that is athirst, come." But there are some so deaf that they cannot hear; others are not thirsty enough—or they think they are not. I have seen men in our after-meetings with two streams of tears running down their cheeks; and yet they said the trouble with them was that they were not anxious enough. They were anxious to be anxious. Probably Christ saw that men would say they did not feel thirsty; so He told the apostle to make the invitation still broader. So the last invitation let down into a thirsty world is this: "Whosoever will, let him take the water of life freely" (Revelation 22:17).

Thank God for those words "Whosoever will"! Who will come and take it? That is the question. You have the power to accept or to reject the invitation. A man in one meeting once was honest enough to say "I won't." If I had it in my power I would bring this whole audience to a decision now, either for or against. I hope many now reading these words will say, "I will!" If God says we can, all the devils in hell cannot stop us. All the infidels in the world cannot prevent us. That little boy, that little girl, can say, "I will!" If it were necessary, God would send down a legion of angels to help you; but He has given you the power, and you can accept Christ this very minute if you are really in earnest.

Let me say that it is the easiest thing in the world to become a Christian, and it is also the most difficult. You will say: "That is a contradiction, a paradox." I will illustrate what I mean. A little nephew of mine in Chicago, a few years ago, took my Bible and threw it down on the floor. His mother said, "Charlie, pick up your uncle's Bible!" The little fellow said he would not. "Charlie, do you know what that word means?" She soon found out that he did, and that he was not going to pick up the Book. His will had come right up against his mother's will.

I began to be quite interested in the struggle; I knew if she did not break his will, he would someday break her heart. She repeated, "Charlie, go and pick up Uncle's Bible, and put it on the table." The little fellow said he could not do it. "I will punish you if you do not." He saw a strange look in her eye, and the matter began to get serious. He did not want to be punished, and he knew his mother would punish him if he did not lift the Bible. So he straightened every bone and muscle in him, and he said *he could not do it.* I really believe the little fellow had reasoned himself into the belief that he could not do it.

His mother knew he was only deceiving himself; so she kept him right to the point. At last he went down, put both his arms around the Book, and tugged away at it; but he still said he could not do it. The truth was—he did not want to. He got up again without lifting it. The mother said, "Charlie, I am not going to talk to you anymore. This matter has to be settled; pick up that Book, or I will punish you." At last she broke his will, and then he found it as easy as it is for me to turn my hand. He picked up the Bible, and laid it on the table.

So it is with the sinner; if you are really willing to take the Water of Life, *you can do it.*

"I heard the voice of Jesus say,
'Come unto Me, and rest;
Lay down, thou weary one, lay down:
Thy head upon My breast.'
I came to Jesus as I was—
Weary, and worn, and sad,
I found in Him a resting-place,
And He has made me glad.

"I heard the voice of Jesus say,
'Behold, I freely give
The living water—thirsty one,
Stoop down, and drink, and live.'
I came to Jesus, and I drank
Of that life-giving stream;
My thirst was quenched, my soul revived
And now I live in Him.

"I heard the voice of Jesus say,
'I am this dark world's Light:
Look unto Me, thy morn shall rise,
And all thy day be bright.'
"I looked to Jesus, and I found
In Him my Star, my Sun;
And in that Light of life I'll walk
Till traveling days are done."

Dr. H. Bonar

*Gospel Dialogue*

# 1

# WHAT IT IS TO BE A CHILD OF GOD

**Mr. Moody and Rev. Marcus Rainsford**

**Mr. Moody:** What is it to be a child of God? What is the first step?

**Rev. M. Rainsford:** Well, sir, I am a child of God when I become united to the Son of God. The Son of God prayed that all who believed upon Him should be one with Him, as He was one with the Father. Believing on Jesus, I receive Him, and become united to Him; I become, as it were, a member of His Body. I am an heir of God, a joint heir with Christ.

**Mr. M.:** What is the best definition of faith?

**Mr. R.:** Trust in the Son of God as the Savior He has given to us. Simple trust, not only in a creed but in a Person. I trust my soul to Him; I trust the keeping of my soul to Him. God has promised that whosoever trusts Him, mercy shall compass him on every side.

**Mr. M.:** Does not the Scripture say that the devils believe?

**Mr. R.:** They believe the truth, do they not? They believe that Jesus was manifested to destroy them; and they "tremble." I wish we

believed as truly and as fully that God sent His
Son into the world to save us.

**Mr. M.:** What is it to "trust"?

**Mr. R.:** I take it to mean four things:

1. Believing on Christ; that is, taking Him at
   His Word.
2. Hoping in Christ; that is, expecting help
   from Him, according to His Word.
3. Relying on Christ; that is, resting on Him
   for the times, and ways, and circum-
   stances in which He may be pleased to
   fulfill His promises according to His
   Word.
4. Waiting on Christ; that is, *continuing* to
   do so, notwithstanding delay, darkness,
   barrenness, perplexing experiences, and
   the sentence of death in myself. He may
   keep me waiting awhile (I have kept Him
   a long time waiting); but He will not
   keep me waiting always. Believing in
   Him, hoping in Him, relying upon Him,
   and waiting for Him—I understand to be
   trusting in Him.

**Mr. M.:** Can all these friends here believe
the promises?

**Mr. R.:** The promises are true, whether we
believe them or not. We do not make them
true by believing them. God could not charge
me with being an unbeliever, or condemn me

for unbelief, if the promises were not true for me. I could in that case turn around and say: "Great God, why did you expect me to believe a promise that was not true for me?" And yet the Scriptures set forth unbelief as the greatest sin I can continue to commit.

**Mr. M.:** How are we "cleansed by *the Blood*?"

**Mr. R.:** "The blood is the life." The sentence upon sinners for their sin was, "The soul that sinneth, it shall die." That we might not die, the Son of God died. The blood is the poured-out life of the Son of God, given as the price, the atonement, the substitute, for the forfeited life of the believer in Jesus Christ. Any poor sinner who receives Christ as God's gift is cleansed from all sin by His blood.

**Mr. M.:** Was the blood shed for us all?

**Mr. R.:** [Let me quote the hymn:]

"There is a fountain filled with blood,
Drawn from Immanuel's veins;
And sinners plunged beneath that flood,
Lose all their guilty stains.

"The dying thief rejoiced to see
That fountain in his day;
And there may we, though vile as he,
Wash all our sins away."

**Mr. M.:** Some may think that this is only a hymn, and that it is not Scripture. Did the Lord ever say anything similar to what the hymn says?

**Mr. R.:** He said: "I have given you the blood upon the altar to make an atonement for your souls." That was said of the picture of the blood of Christ. And at the Last Supper our Lord said His blood was the "blood of the new testament, which is shed for many for the remission of sins."

**Mr. M.:** What is "the gift of God"?

**Mr. R.:** There are three great gifts that God has given to us: (1) His blessed Son; (2) the Holy Ghost, "the promise of the Father," that we might understand the unspeakable gift bestowed on us when He gave His Son; and (3) His Holy Word.

The Holy Ghost has inspired the writers of [the Bible] that we may read, and hear, and know the love that God has for us, "in that, while we were yet sinners, Christ died for us" (Romans 5:8). We could not have the Son for our Savior, unless God gave Him. We could not understand the gift of God, unless the Holy Ghost had come to quicken us and teach us; and this He does through the Word.

**Mr. M.:** How much is there in Christ for us who believe?

**Mr. R.:** In Him dwelt "all the fulness of the Godhead bodily" (Colossians 2:9)—fulness of life, of righteousness, of sanctification, of redemption, title to heaven, and fitness for it; all that God wants from us, and all that we want from God, He gave in the person of Christ.

**Mr. M.:** How long does it take God to justify a sinner?

**Mr. R.:** How long? The moment we receive Him we receive authority to enroll ourselves among the children of God, and are then and there justified from all things. The sentence of complete justification does not take long to pronounce. Some persons profess to see a difficulty in the variety of ways in which a sinner is said to be justified before God: (1) justified by God; (2) justified by Christ; (3) justified by His blood; (4) justified by grace; (5) justified by faith; and (6) justified by works.

Justification has reference to a court of justice. Suppose a sinner is standing at the bar of God, the bar of conscience, and the bar of his fellowmen, charged with a thousand crimes.

There is the Judge: that is God, who alone can condemn or justify: "It is God that justifieth." That is *justification by God.*

There is the Advocate, who appears at court for the sinner; the counselor, the intercessor. That is Christ. So we are *"justified by Christ."*

There is next to be considered the ground and reason on account of which the advocate pleads before the judge. That is the merit of Christ's own precious blood. That is *justification by His blood.*

Next, we must remember the law which the judge is dispensing. The law of works? Nay, but the law of grace and faith. That is *justification by His grace.*

And now the Judge Himself pronounces the result. "Be it known unto you . . . that through this Man is preached unto you the forgiveness of sins; and by him all that believe are justified from all things" (Acts 13:38–39). Now for the first time, the sinner at the bar knows the fact. This is *justification by faith.*

[At last] the justfied man leaves the criminal's dock. He does not return to his prison, or to his chains. He walks forth from the courthouse a justified man; and all men, friends or foes, are made aware that he is free. That is *justification by works.*

**Mr. M.:** A man says: "I have not found peace." How would you deal with him?

**Mr. R.:** He is really looking for the wrong thing. I do not look for peace. I look for *Christ;* and I get peace with Him. Some people put peace in the place of Christ. Others put their repentance or prayers in the place of Christ. Anything put in the place of Christ, or between the sinner and Christ, is in the wrong place. When I get Christ, I possess in Him everything that belongs to Him, as my Savior.

**Mr. M.:** Some think they cannot be Christians until they are sanctified.

**Mr. R.:** Christ is my sanctification, as much as my justification. I cannot be sanctified but by His blood. There is a wonderful passage in

Exodus. The high priest there represented in picture the Lord Jesus Christ. There was to be placed on the forefront of the miter of the high priest, when he stood before God, a plate of pure gold, and engraved upon it as with a signet the words: "Holiness to the Lord." My faith sees it on the forefront of the miter on the brow of my High Priest in heaven. "And it shall be upon Aaron's forehead, that Aaron may bear the iniquity of the holy things, which the children of Israel shall hallow in all their holy gifts; and it shall be *always* upon his forehead, that they may be accepted before the Lord" (Exodus 28:38, italics added). That was for Israel of old! That on the brow of Jesus Christ is for me. Yes—for me, "that I may be accepted before the Lord." As I believe this truth it purifies my heart, it operates on my affections and my desires; and I seek to walk with Him, because He is my sanctification before God just as I trust in Him as my justification—because He shed His blood for me.

**Mr. M.:** What is it to believe on His name?

**Mr. R.:** His name is His revealed self. We are informed what it is in Exodus. Moses was on the mount with God, and He had shown him wonderful things of kindness and of love. And Moses said, "O God, show me thy glory!" And He said, "I will make all my *goodness* pass before thee."

So He put Moses in the cleft of the rock,

and proclaimed the name of the Lord: "The Lord, The Lord God, merciful and gracious, longsuffering, and abundant in goodness and truth, keeping mercy for thousands, forgiving iniquity and transgression and sin"—there it is, root and branch—"and that will by no means clear the guilty" (Exodus 34:6–7). That is His name; and His glory He will not give unto another, and to believe in the name of the Lord is just to shelter under His promises.

**Mr. M.:** What is it to "receive the kingdom of God like a little child?"

**Mr. R.:** Well, I do not believe in a little child being an innocent thing. I think it means that we are to receive it in all our need and helplessness. A little child is the most dependent thing on earth. All its resources are in its parents' love; all it can do is to cry; and its necessities explain the meaning to the mother's heart. If we interpret its language, it means: "Mother, wash me; I cannot wash myself. Mother, clothe me; I am naked, and cannot clothe myself. Mother, feed me; I cannot feed myself. Mother, carry me; I cannot walk." It is written, "A mother may forget her sucking child, yet will not I forget thee."

This it is to receive the kingdom of God as a little child: to come to Jesus in our helplessness and say: "Lord Jesus, wash me!" "Clothe me!" "Feed me!" "Carry me!" "Save me, Lord, or I perish."

**Mr. M.:** A good many say they are going to try. What would you say to such?

**Mr. R.:** God wants no man to "try." Jesus has already tried. He has not only tried, but He has succeeded. "It is finished." Believe in Him who has "made an end of sins, making reconciliation for iniquity, finishing transgression, and bringing in everlasting righteousness."

**Mr. M.:** If people say they are "going to try," what would you say to them?

**Mr. R.:** I should say, "Put trust in the place of trying; believing in the place of doubting"; and I should urge them to come to Christ as they are, instead of waiting to be better. There is nothing now between God the Father and the poor sinner, but the Lord Jesus Christ; and Christ has put away sin that I may be joined to the Lord. "But he that is joined unto the Lord is one spirit" (1 Corinthians 6:17); "And where the Spirit of the Lord is, there is liberty" (2 Corinthians 3:17).

**Mr. M.:** About the last thing an anxious inquirer has to contend with is his feelings. There are hundreds here very anxious to know they are safe in the kingdom; but they think they have not the right kind of feeling. What kind of feeling should they have?

**Mr. R.:** I think there are several of those present who can say that they found a blessing in the after-meetings through one verse of Scripture. I will quote it as an answer to your question: "Who is among you that feareth the Lord, that obeyeth the voice of His servant, that walketh in darkness, and hath no light? Let him trust in the name of the Lord, and stay upon his God" (Isaiah 50:10). Some of you may be walking in darkness; that is how you feel. What is God's command? "Let him trust in the name of the Lord, and stay upon his God." If I am to trust God in the darkness, I am to trust Him anywhere.

**Mr. M.:** You would advise them, then, to trust in the Lord, whether they have the right kind of feeling or not?

**Mr. R.:** If I were to think of my feelings for a moment, I should be one of the most miserable men in this hall tonight. My feelings are those of a sinful corrupt nature. I am just to believe what God tells me in spite of my feelings. Faith is "the evidence of things not seen." I might add that it is also "the evidence of things not felt."

**Mr. M.:** Some may say that faith is the gift of God and that they must wait till God imparts it to them.

**Mr. R.:** "Faith cometh by hearing." The Word of God is the medium through which faith comes to us. God has given us Christ, and He has given us His Spirit and His Word; what need is there to wait? God will give faith to the man who reads His Word and seeks for His Spirit.

**Mr. M.:** What, then, should they wait for?

**Mr. R.:** I do not know of anything they have to wait for. God says: "Come now. Believe now." No, no, there is nothing to wait for. He has given us all He has to give, and the sooner we take it the better.

**Mr. M.:** Perhaps some of them think they have too many sins to allow their coming.

**Mr. R.:** The Lord Jesus has put away sin by the sacrifice of Himself. "As far as the east is from the west, so far hath he removed our transgressions from us." Why do we not believe him? He says He has "made an end of sins." Why do we not believe Him? Is He a liar?

**Mr. M.:** Is unbelief a sin?

**Mr. R.:** It is the root of all sin.

**Mr. M.:** Has a man the power to believe these things, if he will?

**Mr. R.:** When God gives a command, it means that we are able by His grace to do it.

**Mr. M.:** What do you mean by "coming" to Christ?

**Mr. R.:** Believing in Him. If I were to prepare a great feast in this hall tomorrow night, and say that any man that comes to it would have a grand feast and a five-pound note besides, there would not be any question as to what "coming" meant. God has prepared a great feast. He has sent His messengers to invite all to come; and there is nothing to pay.

**Mr. M.:** What is the first step?

**Mr. R.:** To believe.

**Mr. M.:** Believe what?

**Mr. R.:** God's invitation; God's promise; God's provision. Let us believe the faithfulness of Him who calls us. Does God intend to mock us, and make game of us? If He did so to one man, it would hush all the harps in heaven.

**Mr. M.:** Suppose the people do "come," and that they fall into sin tomorrow?

**Mr. R.:** Let them come back again. God says we are to forgive till seventy times seven. Do you think the great God will do less than He commands us to do?

**Mr. M.:** If they truly come, will they have the desire to do the things they used to do before?

**Mr. R.:** When a man really receives Christ into his heart, he experiences "the expulsive power of a new affection." The devil may tempt him to sin; but sin has lost its attraction. A man finds out that it does not pay to grieve God's Holy Spirit.

**Mr. M.:** What would you advise your converts to do?

**Mr. R.:** When you were little babes, if you had had no milk, no clothing, and no rest, you would not have lived very long. You are now the result of your fathers' and mothers' care. When a man is born in the family of God he has life; but he needs food. "Man doth not live by bread alone." If you do not feed upon God's promises you will be of no use in God's service; it will be well for you if your life does not die out altogether before long. Then you need exercise. If you only take food, and do no work, you will soon suffer from what I may call spiritual apoplexy. When you get hold of a promise, go and tell it to others. The best way for me to get help for myself is by trying to help others. There is one great promise that young disciples should never forget: "He that watereth shall be watered also himself."

**Mr. M.:** How are they to begin?

**Mr. R.:** I believe there are some rich ladies and rich gentlemen on the platform. When such persons are brought to the Lord, they are apt to be ashamed to speak about salvation to their old companions. If our Christian ladies would go amongst other ladies, and Christian gentlemen amongst gentlemen of their own class, and so on—we should see a grand work for Christ. Each of you have some friends or relations you can influence better than anybody else can. Begin with them; and God will give you such a taste for work that you will not be content to stay at home: you will go and work outside as well.

**Mr. M.:** A good place to start would be the kitchen, would it not? Begin with some little kitchen meetings. Let some of you get fifteen or twenty mothers together; and ask them to bring their young children with them. Sing some of these sweet hymns; read a few verses of Scripture; get your lips opened and you will find that streams of salvation will be breaking out all around. I always think that every convert ought to be good for a dozen others right away.

**Mr. R.:** Let me tell a little incident in my own experience. I was once asked to go and see a great man and tell him about Christ. He did not expect me and if I had known that, perhaps I should not have had the faith to go at all. When I went he was very angry and nearly turned me out of the house. He was an old man and had one little daughter. A few weeks afterward he went to the continent, and his daughter went with him. One day when he was very ill he saw his daughter looking at him, while the tears rolled down her cheeks. "My child," he said "what are you crying about?" "Oh, Papa, you do not love the Lord Jesus Christ; I am afraid you are going to hell!"

"Why do you say that?"

"Do you not remember when Mr. Rainsford called to see you, you were very rude to Him? I never saw you so angry. And he only wished to speak to you about Jesus."

"Well, my child, you shall read to me about Jesus."

If that man has gone to heaven—I do not say whether he has or not—the only light he had he got from his little daughter. You set to work; and you cannot tell what may be the result, by the blessing of God.

> "Sons of God, beloved in Jesus
> Oh, the wondrous word of grace!
> In His Son the Father sees us,
> And as sons He gives us place.
>
> "Blessed power now brightly beaming—
> On our God we soon shall gaze;
> And in light celestial gleaming
> We shall see our Savior's face.
>
> "By the power of grace transforming
> We shall then His image bear;
> Christ His promised word performing,
> We shall then His glory share."
>
> El Nazman

*Gospel Dialogue*

# 2

# HOW TO BECOME A CHRISTIAN

## Mr. Moody and Rev. Marcus Rainsford

**Mr. Moody:** Mr. Rainsford, how can one make room in his heart for Christ?

**Rev. M. Rainsford:** First, do we really want Christ to be in our hearts? If we do, the best thing will be to ask Him to come and make room for Himself. He will surely come and do so. "I can do all things through Christ which strengtheneth me." "Without me ye can do nothing."

**Mr. M.:** Will Christ crowd out the world if He comes in?

**Mr. R.:** He spoke a parable to that effect. "When a strong man armed keepeth his palace [the poor sinner's heart], his goods are in peace: But when a stronger than he shall come upon him, and overcome him, he taketh from him all his armour wherein he trusted [unbelief, false views of God, worldliness, and love of sin], and divideth his spoils" (Luke 11:21–22). The devil keeps the heart, because Christ desires it for His throne—until Christ drives Him out.

**Mr. M.:** What is the meaning of the promise "Him that cometh to me I will in no wise cast out" (John 6:37)?

**Mr. R.:** I think we often put the emphasis upon the wrong word. People are troubled about how they are going to come, when they should put the emphasis on Him to whom they are coming. "Him that cometh to me I will in no wise cast out," no matter how he may come. I remember hearing this incident at an after-meeting. A gentleman was speaking to an anxious inquirer, telling him to *come* to Christ, to *trust* in Christ; but the man seemed to get no comfort. He said that was just where he found his difficulty. By and by, another friend came and spoke to the anxious one. All he said was: "Come to *Christ;* trust in *Christ.*" The man saw it in a minute. He went and told the other gentleman, "I see the way of salvation now." "Tell me," said he, "What did that man say to you?" "Well, he told me to trust in Christ." "That is what I told you." "Nay, you bade me *trust* in Christ, and *come* to Christ; he bade me trust in *Christ,* and come to *Christ* ." That made all the difference.

**Mr. M.:** What does Christ mean by the words *"in no wise"*?

**Mr. R.:** It means that if the sins of all sinners on earth and all the devils in hell were upon your soul, He will not refuse you. Not even in the range of God's omniscience is there a reason why Christ will refuse any poor sinner who comes to Him for pardon.

**Mr. M.:** What is the salvation He comes to proclaim and to bestow?

**Mr. R.:** To deliver us from the power of darkness and the bottomless pit, and set us upon the throne of glory. It is salvation from death and hell and curse and ruin. But that is only the half of it. It is salvation to God, and light, and glory and honor, and immortality; and from earth to heaven.

**Mr. M.:** If the friends here do not come and get this salvation, what will be the true reason?

**Mr. R.:** Either they are fond of some sin which they do not intend to give up, or they do *not* believe they are in a lost condition, and under the curse of God, and therefore do not feel their need of Him who "came to seek and to save that which was lost." Or they do not believe God's promises. I have sometimes asked a man, "Good friend, are you saved?" "Well, no, I am not saved." "Are you lost?" "Oh, God forbid! I am not lost." "Where are you, then, if you are neither saved nor lost?" May God wake us up to the fact that we are all in one state or the other.

**Mr. M.:** What if any of them should fall into sin after they have come to Christ?

**Mr. R.:** God has provided for the sins of His people, committed after they come to Christ, as surely as for their sins committed before they came to Him. Christ "ever liveth to make intercession" for all that "come unto God by Him." "If we say that we have no sin, we deceive ourselves, and the truth is not in us. If we confess our sins, he is faithful and just to forgive us our sins, and to cleanse us from all unrighteousness." . . . For, "if any man sin, we have an advocate with the Father, Jesus Christ the righteous. And he is the propitiation for our sins." He will take care of our sinful, tried and tempted selves, if we trust ourselves to Him.

**Mr. M.:** Is it not said that if we sin willfully after we have received the knowledge of the truth, "there remaineth *no more* sacrifice for sins"?

**Mr. R.:** Yes. Paul wrote it in his epistle to the Hebrews (10:26). Some of them were trifling with the blood of Christ, reverting to the types and shadows of the Levitical Law, and trusting to a fulfilled ritual for salvation. He is not referring to *ordinary acts of sin.* By sinning willfully he means, as he explains it, a *treading "under foot the Son of God"* (verse 29), and a total and final apostatizing from Christ. Those who reject or neglect Him will find no other sacrifice for sin remaining. Before Christ came the Jewish ceremonies were shadows of the good things to come; but Christ was the substance of them. But now that He has come to put away sin by the sacrifice of Himself, there is no other sacrifice for sin remaining for those who reject Him. God will send no other Savior, and no further atonement; no second "fountain" shall be opened "for sin and uncleanness." There remains, therefore, nothing for the rejector of salvation by Christ, but "a fearful looking for of judgment" (verse 27).

**Mr. M.:** There are some who say they do not know that they have the right kind of faith.

**Mr. R.:** God does not ask us if we have the right kind of faith. He tells us the right thing to believe, and the right faith is to believe the right thing, even what God has told us and promised us. If I told you, Mr. Moody, that I had found a hymnbook last night you would believe me, would you not? (Mr. Moody: Yes.) Suppose I said it was the valuable one you lost the other night, you would believe me also just the same. There is no difference in the *kind of* faith; the difference is in the thing *believed.* When the Son of God tells me that He died for sinners, that is a fact for my faith to lay hold of: the faith itself is not the thing to be considered. I do not look at my hand when I take a gift, and wonder what sort of a hand it is. I look at the gift.

**Mr. M.:** What about those people who say their hearts are so hard, and they have no love for Christ?

**Mr. R.:** Of course they are hard and cold. No man loves Christ till he believes that Christ loves him. "We love him, because he first loved us." It is the love of God shed abroad in our hearts by the Holy Ghost that makes the change.

**Mr. M.:** Paul said he was "crucified with Christ" (Galatians 2:20). What did he mean?

**Mr. R.:** Oh, that is a grand text. Thank God I have been "crucified with Christ." The Cross of Christ represents the death due to the sinner who had broken God's laws. When Christ was crucified every member of His body was crucified; but every believer that was, or is, or shall be, is a member of Christ's body, of His flesh, and of His bones. Again, we read: "Whether one member suffer, all the members suffer with it; or one member be honoured, all the members rejoice with it. Now ye are the body of Christ, and members in particular" (1 Corinthians 12:26–27). So when Christ was crucified for sin, I was also crucified in Him; and now I am dead and gone—as far as my old self is concerned. I have already suffered for sin in Him. Yes; I am dead and buried with Christ. That is the grand truth that Paul laid hold upon. I am stone dead as a sinner in the sight of God. As it is written, I am "become dead to the law by the body of Christ; that [I] should be married to another, even to him who is raised from the dead, that [I] should bring forth fruit unto God" (Romans 7:4). "I am crucified with Christ: nevertheless I live; yet not I, but Christ liveth in me" (Galatians 2:20); and God Himself commands me so to regard my standing before Him as His believing child. "In that [Christ] died, he died unto sin once; but in that he liveth, he liveth unto God. *Likewise reckon ye also yourselves to be dead indeed unto sin, but*

*alive unto God through Jesus Christ our Lord"*
(Romans 6:10–11, italics added).

**Mr. M.:** Should not a man repent a good
deal before he comes to Christ?

**Mr. R.:** "Repent a good deal"! I do not
think any man repents in the true sense of the
word till he loves Christ and hates sin. There
are many false repentances in the Bible. We are
told that Pharaoh repented when the judgment of God came upon him, and he said, "I
have sinned"; but as soon as the judgment
passed away, he went back to his sin. We read
that Balaam said: "I have sinned." Yet he "loved
the wages of unrighteousness." When Saul lost
his kingdom he repented; "I have sinned," he
said. When Judas Iscariot found that he had
made a great mistake, he said: "I have sinned in
that I have betrayed the innocent blood." Yet
he went "to his own place." I would not give
much for these repentances; I would rather
have Peter's repentance: when Christ looked
upon His fallen saint it broke his heart, and he
went out and wept bitterly. Or the repentance
of the prodigal, when his father's arms were
around his neck and his kisses on his cheek,
and he said, "Father, I have sinned against
heaven, and in thy sight, and am no more worthy to be called thy son."

**Mr. M.:** What is your title to heaven?

**Mr. R.:** The person, the life, death, and

righteousness of the God-man, the Son of God, my Substitute, and my Savior.

**Mr. M.:** How do you obtain that?

**Mr. R.:** By receiving Him. "As many as received him, to them gave He [authority] to become the sons of God, even to them that believe on his name."

**Mr. M.:** What is your fitness for heaven?

**Mr. R.:** The Holy Spirit dwelling in my heart is my fitness for heaven. I have only to get there; and I have, by this great gift, all tastes, desires, and faculties for it. I have the eyes to contemplate it; I have the ears for heaven's music; and I can speak the language of the country. The Holy Spirit in me is my fitness and qualification for the splendid inheritance for which the Son of God has redeemed me.

**Mr. M.:** Would you make a distinction between Christ's work for us and the Spirit's work in us?

**Mr. R.:** Christ's work for me is the payment of my debt; the giving to me a place in my Father's home, the place of sonship in my Father's family. The Holy Spirit's work in me is to make me fit for His company.

**Mr. M.:** You distinguish, then, between the work of the Father, the work of the Son, and the work of the Holy Spirit.

**Mr. R.:** Thanks be to God. I have them all, and I want them all—Father, Son, and Holy Ghost. I read that my heavenly Father took my

sins and laid them on Christ; "The Lord hath
laid on him the iniquity of us all" (Isaiah 53:6).
No one else had a right to touch them. Then I
want the Son, who "his own self bare [my] sins
in his own body on the tree" (1 Peter 2:24).
And I want the Holy Spirit. I should know nothing about this great salvation, and care nothing
for it, if the Holy Spirit had not come and told
me the story, and given me grace to believe it.

**Mr. M.:** What is meant when we are told
that Christ saves "to the uttermost"?

**Mr. R.:** That is another grand truth. Some
people are troubled by the thought that they
will not be able to hold out if they come to
Christ. There are so many crooked ways, pit-
falls, and snares in the world; there is the
power of the flesh and the snare of the devil.
So they fear they will never get home. The idea
of the passage is this. Suppose you are on the
top of some splendid mountain, very high up.
You look away to where the sun sets, and you
see many a river, and many a country, and
many a barren waste between. Christ is able to
save you through and over them all, out and
out, and beyond—to the uttermost.

**Mr. M.:** Suppose a man came in here just
out of prison: all his life he has been falling,
falling, till he has become discouraged. Can
Christ save him all at once?

**Mr. R.:** It is just as easy for Christ to save a
man with the weight of ten thousand sins upon

him and all his chains around him, as to save a
man with one sin. If a man has offended in one
point, the Scripture says he is guilty of all.

**Mr. M.:** If a man is forgiven, will he go out
and do the same thing tomorrow?

**Mr. R.:** Well, I hope not. All I can say is that
if we do, we shall smart for it. I have done many
a thing since the Lord revealed Himself to my
soul that I should not have done—I have gone
backward and downward, but I have always found
that it does not pay when I do anything that
grieves my heavenly Father. I think He sometimes allows us to taste the bitterness of what it
is to depart from Him. And this is one of the
many ways by which He keeps us from falling.

**Mr. M.:** What do you consider to be the
great sin of sins?

**Mr. R.:** The Word of God tells us that there
is only one sin of which God alone can convince us. If I cut a man's throat or if I steal, I do
not need God to convince me that that is a sin.
But it takes the power of the Holy Ghost to convince me that not to receive Christ, not to love
Christ, not to believe in Christ, is the sin of sins,
the root of sins. Christ says, "When [the Spirit]
is come, He will reprove the world of sin, . . .
*because they believe not on me*" (John 16:8,9).

**Mr. M.:** What do you mean by "the Word of
God"?

**Mr. R.:** The Son of God is the Word of God
incarnate; the Bible is the Word of God written.

The one is the Word of God in my nature; the other is the Word of God in my language.

**Mr. M.:** If a man receives the Word of God into his heart, what benefit is it to him, right here now?

**Mr. R.:** The Father and the Son will make their abode with him, and he will be the temple of the Holy Ghost. Where He goes, the whole Trinity goes; and all the promises are his. "Man shall not live by bread alone, but by every word that proceedeth out of the mouth of God."

**Mr. M.:** Who is it that judges a man to be unworthy of eternal life?

**Mr. R.:** *Himself!!* There is a verse in Acts 13 that is worth remembering: "Seeing ye put it [the Word of God] from you, and judge yourselves unworthy of everlasting life, lo, we turn to the Gentiles" (verse 46). God does not judge us unworthy. He has given His Son for our salvation. When a man puts away the Word of God from him and refuses to receive Christ into his heart, he judges himself unworthy of salvation.

**Mr. M.:** I understand, then, that if a man rejects Christ tonight, he passes judgment on himself as unworthy of eternal life?

**Mr. R.:** He is judging himself unworthy, while God does not so consider him. God says you are welcome to eternal life.

**Mr. M.:** If anyone here wants to please God tonight, how can he do it?

**Mr. R.:** God delights in mercy. Come to

God and claim His mercy in Christ, and you will delight His heart.

**Mr. M.:** Suppose a man says he is not "elected"?

**Mr. R.:** Do you remember the story of the woman of Canaan? Poor soul; she had come a long journey. She asked the Lord to have mercy on her afflicted child. He wanted to try her faith, and He said: "I am not sent but unto the lost sheep of the house of Israel." That looked as if He Himself told her that she was not one of the elect. But she came and worshipped Him, saying, "Lord, help me!" and He helped her there and then. (Matthew 15:24–28) No, there is no election separating between the sinner and Christ.

**Mr. M.:** Say that again.

**Mr. R.:** *There is no election separating the sinner from Christ.*

**Mr. M.:** What is there between the sinner and Christ?

**Mr. R.:** Mercy!! Mercy!!

**Mr. M.:** That brings me near to Christ?

**Mr. R.:** So near that we cannot be nearer. But we must claim it. In John we get God's teaching about election. "This is the Father's will which hath sent me, that of all which he hath given me I should lose nothing, but should raise it up again at the last day" (John 6:39). He will do His work; you may depend upon it. Then in the next verse we read: "And this is the will of him that sent me, that every one which seeth the Son, and believeth on him, may have everlasting life: and I will raise him up at the last day." That is the part I am to take, and when I am done I shall know the Father's will concerning me.

**Mr. M.:** What do you mean by "the new birth"?

**Mr. R.:** I judge it by what I know of the old birth. I was born of human parents into the human family, so I belong to Adam's race by nature and by generation, and I inherit Adam's sin and curse accordingly. The new birth is from union—union by faith with the second Adam; but this is by *grace, not* nature, and when I receive the Lord Jesus Christ I am born of God—not by generation, but by regeneration. As I am united to the first Adam by nature and generation, so I am united by faith through grace and regeneration to the second Adam and inherit all His fullness accordingly.

**Mr. M.:** What is the meaning of being "saved by the blood"?

**Mr. R.:** A gentleman asked me that in the inquiry-room: "What do you mean by the blood?" It is the poured-out life of the Son of God—forfeited as the atonement for sinners' sins.

**Mr. M.:** Is it available now?

**Mr. R.:** Yes, as much as ever it was.

**Mr. M.:** You mean it is just as powerful

today as it was eighteen hundred years ago when He shed it?

**Mr. R.:** If the blood of Abel cried out for vengeance against his slayer, how much more does the blood of Christ cry out for pardon for all who plead it! "It cleanseth [present tense] from all sin."

**Mr. M.:** How do you get faith?

**Mr. R.:** By hearing God's Word. "Faith cometh by hearing, and hearing by the word of God" (Romans 10:17).

**Mr. M.:** How do you get the Holy Spirit?

**Mr. R.:** In the same way as you get faith. The Holy Spirit uses the Word as the chariot by which He enters the believer's soul. The Gospel is called "the ministration of the Spirit."

**Mr. M.:** Is the Word of God addressed to all here?

**Mr. R.:** "He that hath an ear, let him hear what the Spirit saith unto the churches" (Revelation 3:22).

**Mr. M.:** What is the Gospel?

**Mr. R.:** "Good tidings of great joy, which shall be to all people" (Luke 2:10). If our Gospel, proclaiming life, pardon, and peace, is not as applicable for salvation to the vilest harlot here as to the greatest saint in London, it is not Christ's Gospel we preach.

**Mr. M.:** What reason does the Scripture give for the Gospel being hid to some?

**Mr. R.:** It is "hid to them that are lost: in

whom the god of this world hath blinded the minds of them which believe not, lest the light of the glorious gospel of Christ, who is the image of God, should shine unto them" (2 Corinthians 4:3–4). May God open all our eyes and take away the veil of unbelief with which the devil may be blinding any of us!

**Mr. M.:** Are there not many who give an intellectual assent to all these things, and who yet have no power and no divine life?

**Mr. R.:** An intellectual assent is not faith. I have never found anyone who really believed God's Word who did not get power in believing it. People may *assent* to it, but I do not admit that that is believing it. I do not think there is any man or woman here who really believes the Gospel of the grace of God, who has not been taught it by the Holy Spirit. I could easily cross-examine any one of those "intellectual believers," who imagines he believes God, but really does not, and he would break down in a few minutes.

**Mr. M.:** For whom, then, did Christ die?

**Mr. R.:** For "the ungodly."

**Mr. M.:** Why is salvation obtained by faith?

**Mr. R.:** That it might be by grace. "Therefore it is of faith, that it might be by grace" (Romans 4:16).

**Mr. M.:** How may a man know if he has eternal life?

**Mr. R.:** By *not* treating God as if He were a

liar, when He tells us He has given us eternal life in His Son.

**Mr. M.:** What is the means by which the New Birth we were speaking of is effected?

**Mr. R.:** "Of his own will begat he us with the word of truth." "Being *born* again, not of corruptible seed, but of incorruptible, by the *word of God* . . . and this is the word which by the gospel is preached unto you" (James 1:18, 1 Peter 1:23, 25, italics added).

> "Oh, the wondrous love of Jesus
> To redeem us with His blood!
> Through His all-atoning merit,
> He has brought us near to God:
> For the boundless grace that saves us
> We His name will magnify;
> He is coming in His glory,
> We shall see Him by and by!
>
> "Oh, the wondrous love of Jesus
> To redeem our souls from death!
> We will thank Him, we will praise Him,
> While His mercy lends us breath:
> We are waiting—only waiting—
> Till He comes our souls to bear
> To the Home beyond the shadows,
> In His Kingdom over there!"
>
> F. J. Croson

*Gospel Dialogue*

# 3

## WHAT IT MEANS TO BE CONVERTED

### Mr. Moody and Mr. Radstock

**Mr. Moody:** Christ says, "Except ye be converted, and become as little children, ye shall not enter into the kingdom of heaven" (Matthew 18:3). What is it to be converted?

**Mr. Radstock:** To be "converted" is to turn to God, who is the only One who can save. We cannot save ourselves even by our religion. Therefore, in order to have salvation we must turn to God, who alone has the grace, the wisdom, and the power to save.

**Mr. M.:** What is it to be born of the Spirit?

**Mr. R.:** Man, by nature, cannot enter into the thoughts of God. He cannot hold communion with God until he has a new nature. The natural man receiveth not the things of the Spirit of God: he has not capacity until he has the new life which God will give him by the power of the Holy Ghost.

**Mr. M.:** Can he get that today if he repents?

**Mr. R.:** Yes. Repentance means a change of mind—a turning away from his own thoughts to hear the voice and the message of God. If we listen to the voice of God and confess our sins, God is "faithful and just to forgive us our sins."

**Mr. M.:** To whom are we to confess our sins?

**Mr. R.:** When the light of God comes in, we see then we are guilty before Him; then we are constrained to go and lay our case before Him. If we confess our sins, He is faithful and just to forgive us.

**Mr. M.:** There is a passage that says the Lord Jesus Christ bears our sins. In what sense did He bear our sins?

**Mr. R.:** The Lord Jesus Christ had really laid to His charge sins which He had never committed. He was punished as if He had been the sinner. Therefore on the cross He cried out, "My God, my God, why hast Thou forsaken me?" God was dealing with Jesus as if He had really been the guilty one.

**Mr. M.:** Do we get any help by believing that?

**Mr. R.:** When I believe God's testimony, God's witness about Jesus, I then can trust myself to God. Giving myself to God, God becomes my Savior.

**Mr. M.:** Have these friends the power to believe?

**Mr. R.:** They are commanded to believe. They can believe it just as well as they can believe any other fact, if they only listen to God's voice. But they must get rid of their own thoughts and listen to God. Hearing His voice they will believe. "Faith cometh by hearing, and hearing by the word of God."

**Mr. M.:** All the sinner has to do is to repose in the promises of God?

**Mr. R.:** Simply to trust himself to God.

**Mr. M.:** What would you say to a man who says he has tried a good many times and failed, and who has become discouraged?

**Mr. R.:** That man has probably made a good many resolutions, hoping that he would gradually make himself a Christian by going through this or that process or by doing this or that thing. Of course he failed because he tried to make himself a Christian. Instead of trying to save himself, let him trust in God, who has pledged His word that everyone who believes on the Lord Jesus Christ has at that moment everlasting life.

**Mr. M.:** Should a man not break off from some of his sins before he comes to God? Suppose he swears or has a bad temper, should he not get a little control over his temper, or stop swearing, before he comes to Christ?

**Mr. R.:** God knows that a man's nature is wrong; therefore, He has promised to give a man a new nature. We must therefore go to God, just as a man goes to a physician because he needs to be cured of some disease.

**Mr. M.:** Can a drunkard or a blasphemer be saved all at once?

**Mr. R.:** Paul says: "To him that worketh not, but believeth on him that justifieth the ungodly"

—bad people, lost people, ruined people—"his faith is counted for righteousness" (Romans 4:5). When he believes God, God becomes his Savior. God is the friend of sinners.

**Mr. M.:** What is it to believe God?

**Mr. R.:** To take Him at His word.

**Mr. M.:** Do you not think there are a good many here who believe that Jesus Christ is the Savior of the world and yet they are not saved?

**Mr. R.:** No doubt; because they have not believed for themselves. A man at the time of the Deluge, for instance, might have said, "Yes, I believe it is a very good ark indeed, and that it will save those who get into it." But it does not follow that he got into it himself. The ark only saved those who went into it. So when a man trusts in Jesus Christ for himself, Jesus becomes his personal and eternal Savior.

**Mr. M.:** What if he should fall into sin after he has believed in Christ?

**Mr. R.:** "These things write I unto you, that ye sin not," says John. "And if any man sin, we have an advocate with the Father" (1 John 2:1). The Good Physician will not give up His case because of the disease; He will deal with it. The Good Shepherd will not turn his poor wandering sheep away; He will go after it, and bring it back. He has promised that He will save His people from their sins.

**Mr. M.:** Is salvation within the reach of every man here tonight?

**Mr. R.:** Jesus said, "God so loved the world, that he gave his only begotten Son, that *whosoever* believeth in him should not perish, but have everlasting life."

**Mr. M.:** But some say they do not feel that; they do not realize it.

**Mr. R.:** When they take God at His word, and cast themselves upon Him, whether they feel it or not—when they confess Jesus Christ as their Lord—the Holy Spirit will come as a power to make them realize it. For instance, a man at the time of the Deluge might have stood outside the ark and said, "I cannot realize how this ark will lift me up above the waters." But if he were inside when the flood came he would realize it. The sinner must believe first, and have his experience afterwards. A man is told that a certain train will take him to Edinburgh. He has never been there: he does not understand about this particular train; and he cannot realize that it will take him there. But he knows that he may trust the friend who told him; so he gets into the train. Then he realizes that he is in the train; by and by he will be able to realize that he is in Edinburgh.

**Mr. M.:** Would you advise people to come to God as they are, with their unfeeling, treacherous, hard hearts—with any kind of heart?

**Mr. R.:** God has provided this salvation for lost sinners—those who are thoroughly bad and corrupt. It is for such that God has shown His salvation, His love, His grace.

**Mr. M.:** What would you say to anyone who thinks he has no power to believe?

**Mr. R.:** He *has* the power to believe. Probably he is trying to believe something about himself, to feel something about himself instead of giving credit to God. He is not asked to realize this or that about himself, but to believe the faithful God.

**Mr. M.:** Some say they have no power to overcome a besetting sin.

**Mr. R.:** Jesus came proclaiming liberty to the captives. As we read in the beautiful words of the Church of England Prayer-book: "Though we be tied and bound by the chains of our sin, let the pitifulness of Thy mercy save us." Jesus Christ takes the prisoners of sin and breaks off their chains.

**Mr. M.:** There is something said about "confessing Christ." Would you advise anyone who wants to become a Christian to start right here by confessing Christ with the mouth?

**Mr. R.:** God is already on your side, whoever you are. Christ is Immanuel—God with us and for us. He is already on your side, whether you believe it or not. Now it is for you to decide whether He shall be your Savior. He says that if you own Him as Lord—who is now the One rejected by the world—He is responsible to be your Savior from that moment.